Small Change
A LIFE OF
TOM WAITS

Small Change
A LIFE OF
TOM WAITS

St. Martin's Press
New York

Library of Congress Cataloging-in-Publication Data

Humphries, Patrick.
    Small change : a life of Tom Waits / Patrick Humphries.
        p.   cm.
    ISBN 0-312-04582-4 (pbk. original)
    1. Waits, Tom, 1949–   2. Singers—United States—Biography.
I. Title.
ML420.W13H85   1990
781.64'092—dc20
    [B]
                                                                    90-37199

First published in Great Britain by Omnibus Press

10 9 8 7 6 5 4 3 2

ACKNOWLEDGEMENTS

First off, there's some leviticously, deuteronomous hi-voltage thanks to
Brian Case; Chuck Tatum, RIP; the rarely wrong Fred Dellar; the Jump
Brothers, for the leads; Philip Hall; Pogues Philip Chevron, James Fearnley
and Jem Finer for stolen memories, St Patrick's Night, Brixton 1989; Dan
French; Rob Partridge and Marcia, Island Records coffee and conversation;
John Platt; Peter K. Hogan; Peter O'Brien; Roy Carr ... John Green, Paul
Rayworth and Nigel Simons for Frank's Wild Lunch, March 3, 1989 ... Philip
Norman for his 'Pieces Of Hate'; Russell Ash and Brian Lake for their
'Bizarre Books'.

Thanks too to Kristine McKenna, Gavin Martin, Ted Mico, Chris
Roberts, Jack Barron, John Wilde, Sean O'Hagen, Mike Flood Page, Nick
Kent, Dermot Stokes, Edwin Pouncey, David McGee, Barney Hoskyns, Rip
Rense and Ann Scanlon for their published Tom Waits interviews over the
years.

Sue Parr, as ever, my Jersey Girl 'cos when I'm with her on a Saturday night, don't you know that all my dreams come true? She's also a good dream-weaver the other six nights of the week.

Tom, Tom the Piper's son, he learned to play when he was young ... Tom Traubert, Tom Paxton, Tom Thumb, Tom Verlaine, Thomas Paine, Great Tom, Tom Tyler, Tom Stearns Eliot, Tom, Dick and Harry, Tom Clancy, Tommy Cooper, Dylan Thomas, Doubting Thomas, Thomas More, Tommy Dorsey, Thomas Mann, Tom and Jerry, Tom O'Shanter, Tom Hanks, Thomas de Quincey, Thom Hickey, Uncle Tom (and his Cabin), Thomas Hardy, Tom Selleck, Tomahawk, Tom Conti, Terry Thomas, Thomas the Tank Engine, Tommy Walker, Tom T. Hall, Thomas a'Becket, Tom Berenger, Tommy Gun, Tom Robbins, Thomas Aquinas, Thomas Dylan Brooke, Tomato, Thomas Jefferson, Tom Jones, Tom Dobson, Tom Dooley, Tom Cat, Tom Courtenay, Tombola, Thomas Chatterton, Tom Tiddlers Ground, Tom Robinson, Edward Thomas, Tom Tom Club, Tomboy, Tommy Atkins, Tom Rush, Tom Sawyer.

Thomas Pynchon, Tommy Trinder, Thomas Cranmer, Tom Johnston, Tom Good, Tommy Steele, Thomas Crown (and his affair), Tom O'Connor, Tom Brown (and his schooldays), Tommy Tune, Tom Morphet, Tommy Nutter, Tom Lehrer, Thomas Burberry, Tom Petty, Rufus and Carla Thomas, Tom Cruise, Thomas Dolby, Nicky Thomas, Thomas Tallis, Saint Thomas (and his hospital), George 'Fathead' Thomas, Major Tom.

Tom Fool, Old Tom, Tommy rot, Tom Foolery, Poor Tom, Tom o'Bedlam: A mendicant who levies charity on the plea of insanity ...

Plant ya now, dig ya later ...

6

INTRODUCTION

Growling from the very sole, the voice nags like a hangover; it's a '56 Ford Mercury with a broken exhaust, a silencer that's snapped somewhere on the bayoux. It's a bouncer's roar at closing time, it's New Orleans' given voice. Tom Waits' own favourite description of his tubercular tubes was "Louis Armstrong and Ethel Merman meeting in Hell!"

Hard to believe that Tom Waits could have been any other way. Waits' very public persona has him placed firmly in hazy, after-hours bars, where cool, acoustic jazz percolates through the fug of Marlboro smoke. Jack Kerouac, Nelson Algren, Damon Runyon and Charles Bukowski bellow over a game of craps that's been going on for 20 years. Waits is the crumpled bum in the corner, slumped over a piano that's seen better days; so's the player. His suit looks like it's been squatted in by a gang of Chinese coolies. His ashtray's overflowing, there's a yellow legal-pad of scraps of songs, Waits looks like he's been there all his life, like daylight's just a bad rumour and all his tomorrows are buried at the bottom of a bottle of Bushmills.

Waits comes across as the sort of character Marlon Brando's daddy warned him against in *Guys And Dolls*: "Son, no matter how far you travel, or how smart you get, always remember this: Some day, somewhere, a guy is going to come to you and show you a nice brand-new deck of cards on which the seal is never broken, and this guy is going to offer to bet you that the jack of spades will jump out of this deck and squirt cider in your ear. But, son, do not bet him, for as sure as you do you are going to get an ear full of cider!" Waits said that Chuck E. Weiss was the sort of guy "who'd sell you a rat's ass for a wedding ring; and I'm the sort of guy who'd order a dozen of 'em."

Tom Waits as Beat bum was a persistent image, and one that Waits now shucks, but from early on Tom Waits has been an able self-publicist, creating an image of bar-room soak, a soused spinner of yarns which he carried on off-stage as successfully as on. Curiously, when not promoting himself to the hilt, Waits is a shy character, self-effacing and withdrawn.

8

The Waits I met in London, when he was on parole from Francis Ford Coppola's *One From The Heart*, was a courteous, eloquent man with a pair of the spindliest hands I've ever seen. I ended up chauffeuring him round bits of London I thought he'd like, pointing out the Imperial War Museum in Lambeth, the site of the original Bedlam, where 18th Century aristocrats would pay to watch the hapless lunatics cavort ("This part of town called Bedlam?" asked Waits with wide-eyed interest. He had, after all, once claimed to have rented an apartment on the corner of Bedlam and Squalor).

Lunch at the Charles Dickens at St Katharine's Dock was not for Tom; Filipino waitresses fussed over fish ("What kind of plaice is this?" he asked), he wanted a fish without bones, impossible countered the waitress, but she could offer fish with bones that the diner could remove himself. "But I want something that's never had a bone in it ..." Between this war of attrition, Waits was effusive in his praise for Coppola, and spoke fondly of his wife of seven months Kathleen ("She was going to be a nun, but she married me, so you could say I saved her from the Lord"). We touched on the popularity of women newsreaders ("People always prefer bad news out of a pretty mouth").

Waits was fascinated by Jack The Ripper and the Elephant Man's skeleton. He evinced interest in the forthcoming Royal nuptials between shy Di and the man whose name will one day be on every pillar box in the country ("She still a virgin? There gonna be a celebration of the Royal screwing on their honeymoon?").

The fish hovered like Banquo's Ghost ("Knew a teacher once, choked to death on a fishbone") – John Dory attracted him, I filled in with scant Biblical knowledge, wherein Christ was on the bum in Galilee and cooked fish for the disciples, the fish he chose was John Dory, so legend has it that the distinctive markings represent the place where the Son of God held the fish prior to cooking ("So 'John Dory grilled in lemon sauce' ... you reckon it was grilled by the Son of God?").

Sitting and talking with the writer who had composed some of the most affecting songs of the seventies was a delight. Not for Waits the easy option of crouching behind a barricade of 'The Artist', he graciously undertook a canter through any song I expressed an interest in, was charming, witty and concerned in just the right measure. Since then he's gone on to become a cult hero around the world, one of rock music's more unlikely heroes, a craftsman reared on Gershwin and Cole Porter; Kerouac and Bukowski. He's become one of the few people from the rock orbit to make a successful transition into film acting, his fits and starts film career capped by a powerful performance alongside Oscar winners Jack and Meryl in the otherwise lamentable *Ironweed*. Then there's his albums, from the bar balladry of his début 'Closing Time', through the sustained narrative eloquence of his masterpiece 'Small Change' to the iconoclastic trilogy of the eighties – 'Swordfishtrombones', 'Rain Dogs' and 'Frank's Wild Years'.

9

Waits has been hailed by Elvis Costello and The Pogues, seen his songs covered by the likes of Bruce Springsteen, The Eagles, Marianne Faithfull, Tim Buckley, Paul Young and Bette Midler and throughout it all, kept his sense of humour sharper than a samurai's sword. Waits has delivered more one-liners than the White Star line and from being the bastard son of Sam Spade and Sky Masterson has grown into a happily married father of two with his name in lights.

As a performer, Waits was fun when we needed it. The first time I ever saw him was on the BBC's 'adult' rock programme *The Old Grey Whistle Test* in 1976. This was before punk had broken through, and the show's presenter 'Whispering' Bob Harris sat and introduced a series of 'progressive rock' groups with long hair, bell-bottoms and serious demeanours that fell into two categories: (1) Bands who thought Alec Douglas-Home was still Prime Minister and whose sole entreatment was 'Let's booooooooogie ...' and (2) Dole-faced individuals (all of whom had done National Service with Gong) plucking noises out of guitars and keyboards that sounded like the soundtrack to a cat-stranglers' convention.

Bob clearly didn't know what had hoved into view when he introduced Tom Waits. The shock was, in Vivian Stanshall's immortal phrase, "like being handed a saveloy, blindfold, at a gay party." Waits wheezed through a majestic 'Tom Traubert's Blues' and moved on to 'The Piano Has Been Drinking'. Who was that guy? Here was pathos and wit, here was someone who looked as though he'd picket an Emerson, Lake and Palmer concert, and who sounded like he hadn't slept since 1959.

Tom Waits became a minor obsession. I'd fillet his interviews for one-liners I could use, get maudlin late at night with 'Small Change' and bore everyone rigid with my proselytising on his behalf. Waits seemed to offer some sort of truth in his work, his observations of those whose backs had been broken by a society that demanded success and cared little for failures were piteous without appearing pitiable. Waits didn't glorify squalor, he just recognised its existence, and identified with those who had to eke a living out of it. Too many singer-songwriters wrote about society's derelicts, but you got the impression that they were writing after a late-night detour along Skid Row, to observe the bums and hobos from behind the smoked glass of their block-long chauffeured limousine. With Tom Waits, you felt that there was real dirt under his fingernails.

Flipping the coin, I knew Waits was funny; he made me laugh at a time when there wasn't much to laugh at in rock music (always allowing for a Jon Anderson solo album). Waits seemed the sort of guy whose brief in life was to "let me entertain you ..." The quotes came faster than Space

Invaders, the gags flew like Harpo Marx had finally been given voice. Here's the Tom Waits doll, only for older children, wind him up and watch him go, course he may spill a little cigarette ash over your sofa, but he'll keep you in stitches.

Waits moves on, now nearly 20 years into a career that shows no signs of stagnating; critics have tried to pin him down and keep him in one place, but Tom Waits for no man (and that's the first and last time I'll use that line). Determined, like The Beatles in their Hamburg days, to "mak show", Waits interviews should be taken with a truck load of salt, like: "How did I avoid the draft? I was in Israel on a kibbutz. No that's a lie. I was an aide at the White House. I got excused, the way anyone would get a note from school 'Dear Mr President, Tom is sick today and won't be able to come along …'"

He can be irredeemably irritating, or poetically eloquent in his efforts to elucidate the process: "My memory isn't a source of pain. Parts of it are like a pawnshop, other parts are like an aquarium and other parts are like a closet. I think there's a place where your memory becomes distorted like a funhouse mirror and that's the area I'm most interested in."

Writing a book about Tom Waits was more fun than I had any right to expect, I just hope some of that fun comes across in the text. Asking Tom Waits about his past is like asking for Nero's views on urban redevelopment, both adopt a scorched earth policy. I've done my best to sift through the ashes of Waits' life, from what he told me, and what he told other journalists.

If there's a reliance on verbatim quotes from Waits, it's not laziness on my part. The man is just so damn quotable! To filch a Waits analogy: researching his life and music was like playing one of those crane machines at the fairground; you pay your money, but instead of the cheap sweets and charm bracelets you usually end up with, this time around, the crane picks you up gold, frankincense and just a smattering of myrrh.

That is why I describe *Small Change* as "a life of Tom Waits", there's plenty more life in the old Rain Dog yet. This is just where he's been.

"Do you always lie?" "No, no, I always tell the truth, except to policemen. It's an old reflex."

11

"Talking about what you do is always so difficult. It's like a blind man trying to describe an elephant. You usually make most of it up." Thanks Tom, here's an elephant ...

CHAPTER ONE

13

"... I shambled after them as I've been doing all my life after people who interest me, because the only people for me are the mad ones, the ones who are mad to live, mad to talk, mad to be saved, desirous of everything at the same time, the ones who never yawn or say a commonplace thing, but burn, burn, burn like fabulous yellow Roman candles exploding like spiders across the stars and in the middle you see the blue centrelight pop and everybody goes 'Awww!'"
Jack Kerouac, *On The Road*, Viking, 1957.

Squinting at you from beneath a battered fedora, this is the way Waits tells it: "I was born in the back seat of a Yellow Cab in a hospital loading zone and with the meter still running. I emerged needing a shave and shouted 'Times Square, and step on it!'"

More prosaically, Thomas Alan Waits first cast a cautious eye at the world on December 7, 1949. Truman was in the White House, radios built like mahogany sideboards played cosy songs like 'Buttons And Bows' and

'Baby, It's Cold Outside'. The world had indeed been saved for democracy, but just try getting a decent pair of shoes.

For all Americans of that era, December 7 was, according to President Roosevelt, "a day that shall live in infamy." The infamy though had nothing to do with Mr and Mrs Waits of Pomona, California, or their new born son, but referred to the day eight years earlier when Japanese aircraft had screamed out of the sky over Pearl Harbour and forced America to drag itself reluctantly into World War II.

Tom was the Waits' only son (he has two sisters) and after his birth the family kept on the move, shuffling around Southern California while Tom was growing up. The Waits' spent time in San Diego, Laverne, Pomona, Silver Lake and North Hollywood. For a spell, the family settled in Whittier, whose main claim to fame is being the birthplace of one Richard M. Nixon. Indeed on his election to the White House, the town intended honouring its favourite son with a Richard M. Nixon Museum, but after Watergate the plans were abandoned and the land turned into a public park.

Both of Tom's parents were teachers, his father taught Spanish at Belmont High School for a while, and the language percolated into the family home. Tom Waits has successfully covered his tracks on his childhood, but by all accounts it was a pretty standard middle class background, although Waits later let slip his role model was Pinocchio!

Waits' parents divorced while he was still at school. He told me: "My own background was very middle class. I was desperately keen to get away. My parents were divorced when I was 10-years-old, my father's been married about three times, and my mother finally re-married a private investigator. I was at home with these three women, my mother and two sisters, and although they were there, I was on my own a lot."

After the Waits' divorce, Tom's mother took the family and settled in National City down near the Mexican border, but the family's earlier peripatetic existence had already given Tom a love of travel, a feel for exotic place names and an appreciation of the enormity and diversity of America.

Tom's family background was mixed. His mother's family were Norwegian, while his father's came from Scottish and Irish stock (Ireland remains Tom's favourite country). His paternal grandfather was christened Jesse Frank Waits, taking his Christian names from the notorious outlaws, the James Brothers. Tom's own father, bear in mind, was called Frank.

Unlike many of his rock contemporaries (Robert Zimmerman, David Jones) Waits didn't need to hijack a hip handle for his professional career. According to 19th Century chronicler Ebenezer Cobham Brewer: "'Waits' ... derive their name from those watchmen of former times called waits who sounded a horn or played a tune to mark the passing hours. Waits were employed at the royal court 'to pipe the watch' and also by town corporations ... Waits duly came to provide a uniformed band for their town for civic occasions, and played to the public at Christmas time ..."

The Pomona Waits' musical background was sparse, the first song Tom remembers hearing was the traditional Dublin ballad 'Molly Malone'. Tom's dad played guitar, and one of his earliest musical memories was of driving with his father while the radio played Mexican music "mariachi, ranchera, romantica." His mother used to sing in "some kind of Andrews Sisters quartet" and Waits also claims to remember "an uncle who played church organ. They were thinking about replacing him because every Sunday there were more mistakes than the Sunday before. It got to the point where 'Onward Christian Soldiers' was sounding more like 'The Rite Of Spring' so finally they had to let him go."

Growing up always on the move, his parents divorced before he was into his teens, perhaps it was not that surprising that Tom forged an early bond with the bard of the Beats, that "sad, strange, solitary Catholic mystic," Jack Kerouac.

"I guess everybody reads Kerouac at some point in their life. Even though I was growing up in Southern California, he made a tremendous impression on me. It was 1968. I started wearing dark glasses and got myself a subscription to *Down Beat* ... I was a little late, Kerouac died in 1969 in St Petersburg, Florida, a bitter old man."

Asked in later life if Ann Charters' biography – which showed that Kerouac had actually spent much of his life in his mother's parlour – hadn't pricked the myth of the King of the Beats for him, Waits replied: "No, I actually prefer to see the other side. He wasn't a hero who could do no wrong. He saw a lot, got around. He wasn't nearly as mad and impetuous as Neal Cassady."

The stifling conformity of America in the fifties found urgent release in the writings of the Beats, the pent-up rebellion of James Dean and the iconoclasm of the raucous rock 'n' roll roaring out of the radio. It was a mood that spelled 'freedom', and was snatched at by those who saw a future as straight as tram-lines ahead of them, and shucked it.

"The fifties gave us Joe McCarthy, the Korean War and Chuck Berry," Waits told me. "My own background was very middle class. I was desperately keen to get away ... I loved Kerouac since I first discovered him, which was at a time I could have ended up at Lockheed Aircraft, a jewellery store or a gas station, married with three children, lying on the beach ... a lot of Americans went off on the road, just got into a car and drove, for 3000 miles, east or west."

To Kristine McKenna in 1983, Waits wistfully and vividly evoked the influence Kerouac had on him as a teenager: "He had a stool at the bar and nobody sat there except Jack ... He was writing his own obituary from the moment he began, and I think he was tragically seduced by his own destiny – although I'm not really qualified to say ... I enjoy his impressions of America certainly more than anything you'd find in the Reader's Digest. The roar of the crowd in a bar after work; working for the railroad; living in cheap hotels; jazz."

Kerouac, the Boswell of the Beat Generation, whose best writing captured the manic energy, the fire cracker urgency of the Beats, whose speedy prose conveyed the space and the vastness and the potential of an America being slowly suffocated by the grey conformity of the Eisenhower years. In his best works, Kerouac put across an urgency with its roots in jazz and prose Bop, wherein the Road was the key to the Kingdom, and in freewheeling company, it could take you anywhere.

In *Quest For Kerouac* Chris Challis wrote: "American writers have always faced the vastness of their land: Chingachgook and Uncas padding easily, day after day through virgin forest; Huck and Nigger Jim rolling South under the stars on a great natural waterway; Melville's sailors, white and black and red, establishing the Pacific as the furthest reach of America's boundaries. The Beats followed the tradition but on a scale made possible by postwar technology: the Conestoga, raft and sailing ship gave way to the Greyhound, the automobile, the aircraft. The need to communicate the awe remains."

Tom Waits soaked up Kerouac and got soused on Beat mythology; his favourite album of all time remains Kerouac's 1960 'Blues And Haikus' and at his own New York début in the mid-seventies, Waits was proud to include in his band saxophonist Al Cohn who had played on the album. Waits' bond with Kerouac transcended idolatry though, he instinctively identified with that writer's desperate need to escape from the stifling provincialism of middle-class America. Ironically, it was that very provincialism that had nurtured Kerouac, and to which he returned at the end of his life.

17

When Waits began to break in his own right during the early seventies, he defiantly boasted that he had "slept through the sixties." This wasn't just irreverence, this was heresy. The icons and role models of the sixties stretched way into the rock culture of the seventies and beyond, but Waits was typically out of step, determinedly harking back to earlier heroes: "I was kinda lost in the sixties ... I didn't go to San Francisco until the whole love and flowers bit was all over, and when I did go I was looking for the City Lights Bookstore and the ghost of Jack Kerouac."

Certainly Waits' image at the beginning of his career owed more to Beat Bohemian than the prevalent laid-back California chic. As a teenager, Waits took a 1957 Chevrolet station wagon and drove coast to coast, tearing down the tarmac chasing the ghost of Jack Kerouac. The radio blaring, ignoring the psychedelic mayhem of the time, Waits flicked the dial searching for jazz, Country, R&B, Motown. For Little Richard, Howlin' Wolf, Ray Charles, Little Walter, Charlie Rich; voices and sounds which seemed to Waits to have much more to offer than Lothar And The Hand People, Grateful Dead or The Strawberry Alarm Clock.

At high school, aged 15, Waits turned up in a band called The System, their repertoire restricted to R&B favourites of the time – The Temptations and James Brown were highly regarded. By all accounts, the highlight of The System's set was their version of the Godfather of Soul's 'Papa's Got A Brand New Bag'.

Another Waits favourite, or so he told Mike Flood-Page in 1976, was one Lou Short. "I used to listen to a lot of records by a guy called Lou Short. He made a lotta albums in the forties and nobody knew who he was. He used to pay to have them made. But everybody in Baxter, Putnam County knew who he was. And he was the town hypochondriac. I mean, there's a breeze coming up and he's got a little sniffle ... Anyway, the town hypochondriac finally upped and died, and on his tombstone ... it said 'Lou Short Died' and on the bottom it said 'I told you I was sick!'" To this day, Waits retains a fondness for Lou Short's epitaph, and has requested it for his own tombstone.

The need to get away had taken the teenage Tom Waits on the road. He had some fond memories of driving with his dad along the freeways, appreciating even then the sense of freedom that movement gave. Now, on the road again, he began to feel a real connection with the frontier spirit, which was so much a part of American myth.

One particular childhood image remained with Waits well into his adult life: "Burma Shave is an American shaving-cream company, they advertise on the side of the road and they have these limericks which are broken up into different signs, like pieces of a fortune cookie. You drive for miles before you get the full message. 'Please don't ...' five miles, 'Stick your arm out so far ...' another five miles, 'It might go home ...' another five miles, 'In another man's car – Burma Shave!' They reel you in. So when I was a kid I'd see these signs on the side of the road ... and I think it's the name of a town and I ask my dad 'When we gonna get to Burma Shave?'"

Wheels, wheels, Waits always wanted wheels to get him away, to let him escape: "The first car I had was when I was 14. It's kind of an

American tradition. Getting a licence is kind of like a Bar Mitzvah. It's nice to have a car, but in winter you gotta have a heater, especially when it's colder than an American-Jewish princess on her honeymoon." To Peter O'Brien, Waits lovingly recalled his automotive history, lingering over the names, like a litany of old girlfriends: "Had a '56 Ford Mercury, a '55 Buick Roadmaster, a '55 Special, a '55 Buick Century, a '58 Buick Super, a '54 black Cadillac four-door sedan, a '65 Thunderbird, '49 Plymouth, a '62 Comet ..."

But in spite of all the freedom he had tasted on the road, and his apparent unwillingness to tie himself down to respectability and job responsibility, Waits, somewhat surprisingly, soon buckled down to work. His first job was in 1965 and the ensuing years were to be spent washing dishes, servicing toilets and grilling pizzas at Napoleone's Pizza House in National City, a period Waits would later recall on the closing track of his second album 'The Ghosts Of Saturday Night'. All those long nights spent cooking pizzas, overhearing snatches of conversations and watching the characters who drifted through at least gave Waits plenty of time to think and plenty of material for use later on. Emulating the sailors who passed through on shore leave, Waits had himself tattooed, which gave him something to talk about to his mother.

Waits also did a spell as a firefighter, worked in a Bible factory, a car wash, drove an ice cream truck, and filled in as a bartender and doorman. "I once worked in a jewellery store and when I quit I took a gold watch. I figured they weren't gonna give me one 'cause I'd only been with them six months anyway ...!"

Like so many of his generation, it was music which gave Waits the Out. "I can remember working in a restaurant," he recalled years later, "and hearing music come out of the jukebox and wondering how to get from where I was, in my apron and paper hat, through all the convoluted stuff that takes you to where you're coming out of the jukebox."

As a teenager he began writing his own songs on a big old Gibson acoustic guitar, but later switched to the piano, his first being a gift from an old girlfriend: "It had been left in the rain for a year and only played F-sharp." Didn't stop Waits though, just as it hadn't prevented Irving

19

Berlin, America's most revered composer of popular music, who was also only able to muster F-sharp major on a piano keyboard.

Waits soon began playing in small folk and jazz clubs around San Diego. Every singer-songwriter who ever picked up a guitar in the sixties owed a debt to Bob Dylan, except Tom Waits. His line about sleeping through the sixties wasn't bullshit – on his first self-written press release, Waits cited his musical influences as "Mose Allison, Thelonious Monk, Randy Newman, George Gershwin, Irving Berlin, Ray Charles, Stephen Foster, Frank Sinatra." Not names that were picked up or dropped during the hippy-dippy sixties. Waits appreciated from early on the craft that the true professionals put into their songwriting. He recognised the essential skills which lay behind the easy manner in which Lorenz Hart convinced his listeners that 'when love congeals, it soon reveals, the aroma of performing seals'; the technique of Sammy Cahn, Jimmy Van Heusen and others who threw images and metaphors into popular song like engineers fuelling the boiler. But Waits was also in a good position to appreciate the more pragmatic side of that style of songwriting, like Sammy Cahn, who, when asked which came first, the words or the music, replied, "The phone call!"

It was in and around Los Angeles that Tom Waits first began performing professionally. LA has been called a city with all the personality of a paper cup, but like a magnet, Hollywood's dream factory drew writers and playwrights, musicians and composers. Jazzers and bluesmen had long gravitated to the West Coast, and since the first impact of rock 'n' roll, the city had housed a thriving musical community. Waits was only one of thousands of timid troubadours, but he was already out on a limb. Seated at a piano, the young Tom Waits would croon standards like 'Somewhere', Gershwin's 'Summertime' or Irving Berlin's 'Blue Skies', not for Waits distilled Dylan or limp-wristed adolescent anguish. Since he was in his teens Waits had been casting his net further and further afield, and now he was trawling in all sorts of weird and wonderful fish.

Even early on in his career, Waits had begun to see that what came between the songs could be as important as the music. Lenny Bruce's uncompromising albums on Fantasy and the freewheeling raps of Lord Buckley struck a resonant chord in Waits. Both men were iconoclasts, and in their irreverence lay their danger. Buckley had the best waxed moustache outside of Hercule Poirot, a gravel voice and a penchant for black jazz argot which he turned upside down in his nightclub act. From beneath a massive pith helmet ("so necessary in a night club, dear boy") Buckley swooped and soared; acknowledging a fondness for marijuana ("If I wasn't working this joint, I'd be smoking it!") Buckley had laid bare the odium of racism, the madness of nuclear warfare and displayed a love of language which Waits relished. As he was to say later: "Vocabulary is my main instrument."

Buckley's death in 1960 coincided with the rise of 'sick' comic Lenny Bruce, and Tom Waits was not alone in identifying with Lenny's freewheeling routines. Lenny has been commemorated in song by Bob Dylan, Paul Simon and Phil Ochs, on film by Dustin Hoffman and had his performance heisted by amongst others Richard Pryor and Robin Williams.

21

Bruce's background was in jazz and appropriately it was the late Ralph J. Gleason, editor of *Jazz* magazine, who wrote the sleeve notes to 'The Sick Humor Of Lenny Bruce', expanding on Bruce's affinity with the jazzers: "His is a moral outrage and has about it the air of a jazz man. It is strong stuff – like jazz, and is akin to the point of view of Nelson Algren and Lawrence Ferlinghetti as well as to Charlie Parker and Lester Young. Bruce improvises the way a jazz musician does. His routines on this album, for instance, are never done the same way twice but move like a soloist improvising on a framework of chords and melody ... He's a verbal Hieronymous Bosch in whose monologue there is the same urgency as in a Charlie Parker chorus and the same sardonic vitality in his comments as in Lester Young's reflections on a syrupy pop tune."

In these lines can also be found the genesis of Tom Waits' persona. From Buckley he took the voice, from Bruce the style and from Kerouac the attitude. As the sixties ebbed and flowed on a sea of whimsicality and outright farce, Waits found more of substance in the iconoclastic attitudes of the fifties, but the calendar on the wall said 1972. Here was a man out of time, but could Tom Waits seize the time?

THE BIG BREAK (1): Herb Cohen takes time off from managing Frank Zappa, Captain Beefheart, Wild Man Fischer, Tim Buckley, Alice Cooper and The GTOs to catch Hoot Night at the Los Angeles Troubador in 1972. The doorman of LA's Heritage Club takes to the stage to sing a selection of his own songs in a gentle, quietly jazzy voice. Cohen is impressed, and signs Tom Waits to the Asylum label.

THE BIG BREAK (2): Way back, Ben Frank's on Sunset Strip was was where the cool went to calm down. It was the hangout for Lord Buckley, Harry 'The Hipster' Gibson and Lenny Bruce. By the early seventies it was sadder and emptier than an ageing hooker's bank balance, but still it acted as a magnet for those who wanted to capture a bit of its faded glory. Tom Waits is there one night and falls into conversation with Herb Cohen, who promptly signs him to his management roster on the strength of his shoes.

Waits has his own colourful theory about his chosen career, as he told Mike Flood Page in 1976: "I guess I was always interested in music. Actually I sent away. On the back of a matchbook it said: 'Success Without College, send $5 to PO Box 1531 New York, New York'. And they had a whole list of occupations on the inside: TV repairman, washer and dryer salesman, insurance agent, banker, musician ... draft-dodger, homicidal maniac, axe murderer. I just liked the sound of being a musician. So I'm a living example of success without college. The rest is history."

CHAPTER TWO

Début albums are like stray dogs. They can be a damned nuisance, and you can either kick 'em out the way, or invite them into your house, groom them and watch them become part of the family. Once they're safely inside, they may still scratch the furniture, piss on the floor and drive you to distraction, but once they're there, you can't get them out of the house. Début albums are the distillation of the writer's experience to that point, all the overheard snatches of conversation, the road signs and fragments that sizzle on the grill of the writer's imagination.

Such was the importance attached to the credibility of singer-songwriters during the seventies that Neil Young's credit on 'After The Goldrush' to his then-wife Susan for the patches on his jeans went unremarked. For all Bob Dylan's first-footing efforts at rock liberation, with the emergence of the singer-songwriter as a potent force in pop, the style was in bad shape during the early seventies. The will-they, won't-they petulance of Crosby, Stills, Nash, Freeman, Hardy and Willis. The on-off ups and downs of Joni and Jackson and James and Carly and Carole and

Kris and Rita; the dippy hippiedom of John Sebastian, the voice in the wilderness of Tim Buckley and the cosy causticity of Randy Newman ... The sixties still hovered like a tumescent shadow, while 1969's Woodstock was still being celebrated as the gathering of the tribes, 1973 saw the biggest ever rock festival at Watkins Glen, when 600,000 heads gathered to pay homage to The Band, Grateful Dead and Allman Brothers for goodness sake!

In the decade since Dylan had first given singer-songwriters a voice, the genre had become an integral part of American popular music, despite the critics who derided the over-sensitive heart-on-sleeve style of catharsis and the writers' complete inability to communicate with their audience. The problem, so the theory went, was that most first albums draw on the rich vein of experience culled in the days spent paying dues, but by the time of their second and third albums the artists are often so successful that all they can write about are the agonies and isolation of superstardom and the affairs they're having with other singer-songwriters.

The received wisdom of the sixties was handed down as reverentially as Moses' tablets to the early seventies disciples: 'The answer, my friend, is blowin' in the wind' was replaced by the breathless urgency of 'I've got a brand new pair of roller skates'; 'The love you make is equal to the love you take' became the angst-ridden 'It increases my paranoia, like lookin' in my mirror and seein' a police car!'

The presumption of these spoilt superstars that we would be in the least interested in their diary entries was just so much arrogance; their naïve opinions little more than risible. But such was the climate and the general perception of moral bankruptcy among Western governments, that the rock culture still seemed to offer an alternative. Rock lyrics became the notice board on which those too dumb to have opinions of their own pinned their hopes.

Concerts back then seemed to have little to do with an artist attempting to entertain the crowd and increasingly came more to resemble a Papal audience or college lecture. Some fans even brought pen and paper along to take notes. But in spite of all this there was still an undeniable appeal to the singer-songwriter format, which saw the husband

and wife team of James Taylor and Carly Simon become the most
financially successful partnership in showbusiness, eclipsing even the
enormous drawing power of Elizabeth Taylor and Richard Burton.

By 1973 the rock music hierarchy was as established as any mid-
European monarchy. It was, as ever, a year of débuts, and new talent such
as Steely Dan and Queen cut the wax; but the smart money was on a 24-
year-old whose début was greeted from an obscure suburb of New Jersey.
Bruce Springsteen was only one of a dozen 'new Dylans' the period threw
up.

That same year Tom Waits was off the blocks with 'Closing Time'.
Hard to believe now, but back then, critics were betting who of the two
was going to be the next superstar! You get the impression though that if
Tom Waits had become as big as Bruce Springsteen, he really wouldn't
know what to do with such a massive audience, except maybe get them all
to buy him a drink!

'Closing Time' didn't make waves. Waits wasn't comfortable in the
studio: "I've always found it awkward to adjust to the studio – that
knowledge that you've got the same facilities as any other artist at your
disposal – you can go in and make a great album or you can go in and suck
raw eggs."

Even in those pre-salmonella days, suck eggs he didn't. 'Ol' 55', 'I Hope
That I Don't Fall In Love With You', 'Martha' and 'Rosie' are great songs
by anybody's standards. Waits' songs were far from being the maudlin,
self-pitying paeans beloved by his peers, and although his voice had yet to
gain the gravelly quality which would become his hallmark, it was already
distinctly at odds with the mellow crooning of his Californian
contemporaries. David Geffen's Asylum label for whom Waits recorded
until 1980, was the quintessential label for the Golden State, boasting The
Eagles, Joni Mitchell and Jackson Browne on its roster but none of these
artists sounded remotely like Waits.

'Martha' found Waits adopting the character of an old man, bitterly
regretting the lost love of his life and endeavouring after a 40-year hiatus
to see if she still felt the same way about him. Poignant without being
mawkish, the song displayed Waits' ability at tugging at the heartstrings

while tugging the rug from under you: 'Martha? This is old Tom Frost, I am calling long distance, don't worry 'bout the cost.' As if the recipient of a phone call from someone she hadn't heard from in 40 years would worry about the cost!

Sad though that room couldn't be found on the album for an early Waits demo, 'It Looks Like I'm Up Shit Creek Again', a deceptively gentle country-blues number in the style of Hank Williams. But unfortunately a title like that wouldn't have sat easily on the ears of the radio programmers.

Manager Herb Cohen had called in fellow client Jerry Yester to produce Waits' début; Yester was a late arrival in The Lovin' Spoonful but had already served his production apprenticeship with the phenomenally successful MOR group The Association.

Waits however was clearly not happy with the sound of the finished album. Four years after the release of his début he told John Platt of his inability to see eye to eye with Yester: "We were pulling against each other on the first album. If he had his way he would have made it a more folk-based album, and I wanted to hear upright bass and muted trumpet ... I was just a kid in the studio. Jerry had been around the block, he knew what to do, and at the same time he had his own specific ideas. He got very emotionally involved with the whole project, and I was just overwhelmed to be recording at all."

Like Springsteen's début, there was little on 'Closing Time' to suggest the durable and constantly invigorating career which lay ahead for Tom Waits. It's an album heavy on compromise, fashioned out of the contemporary necessity for singer-songwriters to perform against a tasteful and understated soft-rock background. Only the jazzy 'Ice Cream Man' and some of the sporadically bitter, twisted lyrics gave any indication that Tom Waits had more on offer than any one of a dozen denimed, tortured troubadours.

"Harry Dean Stanton once told me he found a copy of my first album across a railroad track. He was in the middle of nowhere shooting a movie and he found this record melted over the tracks. I kinda like that. Nicer place to end up than in a cut-out bin at a record store," Waits told Kristine McKenna.

You'd have needed the foresight of Nostradamus to have predicted Waits' future on the evidence of this début. While 'Closing Time' was on the other side of the tracks from Waits' Asylum labelmates, it was at least in the same town. The album did attract some attention though. *Rolling Stone* compared him with Randy Newman and Loudon Wainwright III, and concluded its review: "Though many will resist Waits' sensibility as too self-indulgent, there is a consistent humour and sense of the absurd in his work that raises it above the level of banal 'kvetching' ... Waits dances on the line between pathos and bathos without going too far in the wrong direction."

The album's sales were limited to immediate family, but Waits found songs from it covered by established acts such as Tim Buckley, Eric Andersen, Lee Hazlewood, Ian Mathews, John Stewart ... and The Eagles. The band who had come to epitomise everything about the breezy Californian lifestyle included Waits' 'Ol' 55' on their 'On The Border' album.

27

The composer was less than enthusiastic about the 'Take It Easy' boys' treatment, as he gleefully recounted to Fred Dellar: "I don't like The Eagles. They're about as exciting as watching paint dry. Their albums are good for keeping the dirt off your turntable and that's about all ... Country-rockers? Those guys grew up in LA and they don't have cowshit on their boots, they just got dogshit from Laurel Canyon. They wouldn't last two minutes in Putnam County that's for sure. If somebody gets shot and killed there on a Saturday night, the Sunday papers say he just died of natural causes."

To promote the album, Waits toured and toured and toured ... Manager Cohen thought his new boy could do with facing the sort of crowds who came to see his top act, Frank Zappa And The Mothers of Invention. However, the pairing was not a success and Waits later described the time spent supporting Zappa as "a nightly experiment in terror." Perhaps not surprisingly, the audiences who came in their thousands to laugh along with Zappa's cynical songs or to marvel at his guitar playing pyrotechnics showed little sympathy for the proto-Beatnik who stumbled on-stage with just his piano for support, and Waits mumbled his bittersweet songs in aircraft hangars to largely uninterested crowds.

The Zappa crowd wasn't the only one to let its antipathy to Waits be known. "For some godforsaken reason I'd been booked to perform at a Gay Liberation Benefit, a real testy audience ... I had to follow Richard Pryor who'd just completed his act by screaming 'Kiss my rich black ass you faggots' and storming off the stage. We-e-ell I was in something of a quandary at that particular point but I went on anyway and started off with – for some reason I'd chosen to perform the old show tune 'Standing On The Corner Watching All The Girls Go By', something sorta told me it might go down well!"

Still trying to build up a following of his own, Waits found himself opening shows for C&W superstar Charlie Rich ("Sure can sing, that sonofabitch"); latter-day Beatle pianist Billy Preston ("A catastrophe," he cheerfully confirmed to me); John Hammond and Jerry Jeff Walker during his apprenticeship. But the worst, the pits, the one that still causes the clammy 3 a.m. terrors was the one Waits told me about in 1981: "I opened a show once for a guy called Buffalo Bob and the Howdy Doody Review. He was like an American children's programme host. We went out on a tour of colleges, and I'd have to do like three matinées for the children and their mothers. He used to call me 'Tommy', I wanted to strangle the sonofabitch ... I hoped he'd die of bone cancer the entire week."

Waits certainly cut an incongruous figure on the rock circuit of the mid-seventies. Audiences whose brains had long since turned to muesli now came only to marvel at spectacle and have what was left of their minds taken to the cosmos – and beyond! They definitely didn't want a down-at-heel pianist with a bone-white face dredging up anecdotes from a downtown bar.

During his long, punishing years of touring, Waits clocked up more miles than a Greyhound bus, and like John Fogerty must have groaned, "Oh Lord, stuck in Lodi again." All those road miles and shows saw crowds merge into one faceless mass. For all the rigours of touring though, the experience did develop Waits into a consummate performer. Hecklers got short shrift ("Your opinions are like assholes, buddy, everybody's got one") and on the road, Waits was able to constantly refuel his fecund imagination.

Pitched waist-deep, Waits dived headlong into the rock 'n' roll lifestyle when he moved into Los Angeles' Tropicana Motel, notorious for the excesses of previous inhabitants like Janis Joplin, Jim Morrison and Alice Cooper. The Tropicana was where touring bands set up camp, then revelled in all the attendant glories of sex and drugs and rock 'n' roll.

Motel life suited Waits; otherwise like he said, "You go away on tour for three months and come back to a fridge that looks like a science experiment." He was a permanent resident at the Tropicana for much of the seventies, it was the base for his increasingly ambitious attacks on the arteries of America. The motel on Santa Monica Boulevard became the closest thing Waits had to a home for many years. From the Tropicana, he ventured out to the bars around Hollywood and Vine, sometimes taking on board the odd glass of stout or pre-prandial sherry; and he became a regular fixture at the Traveller's Café, buttonholing patrons and relishing their tall tales.

In performance, Waits was gaining the reputation of a time-warped Beat, he was living the life he envisaged, just 10 years too late. Appropriately – along with Allen Ginsberg, William Burroughs and Patti Smith – he attended the 1975 New York launch party for Ed Sanders' book *Tales Of Beatnik Glory*. Ginsberg was by that time one of the few authentic Beat survivors; the sixties had not been kind to those manic chroniclers and doers of the fifties: Kerouac had died by his mother's side in 1969, a bitterly disenchanted man who had little in common with the hippies to whom he was a father figure. Neal Cassady, who actually got out and did what Kerouac only chronicled – on one occasion driving from Denver to San Francisco and back, a round trip of 2,894 miles, in an incredible 33 hours – died alone by the rail tracks in early 1968 after years of drug and alcohol abuse.

Tom Waits was only too happy to take up the Beat baton. His own view of America found many echoes in the writings of Jack Kerouac, and he had long drawn on the daemonic energy of *On The Road* and that burning urgency to get out and find what made the country tick, to put a finger on the pulse. Waits' work also found resonance in the lonely paintings of Edward Hopper, whose works always seemed so much emptier when there were people in them; paintings which showed bright oases pitched against the enveloping dark; paintings that demanded to be viewed to the accompaniment of the plaintive, solitary saxophone of John Coltrane.

Waits' style was to Beat as jazz was to beret. Live he either went out solo, with just his piano – on more than one occasion quite literally – for support; or more frequently, accompanied by stand-up bass and drums. Wreathed in cigarette smoke, eyes closed as if in a trance, hands strolling up and down the boulevard of piano keys, hair curling like smoke from a Guy Fawkes bonfire and that voice ... at this stage of his career Waits' voice hadn't yet been shot to Hell by too many Camels, he could still hold a note, even if the note was struggling to get free. He already rasped out his lyrics though, wheezing like air from a punctured balloon.

30

Tom Waits had little in common with other rock 'n' rollers. His image was a topographic ocean away from the bell-bottomed bands who relied chiefly on distance and spectacle for their effect; the only spectacle guaranteed at a Waits show was whether he'd last the evening on his feet.

Sporting a wispy goatee beard, his extraordinary alabaster hands weaving round the microphone like a tick-tack man, Waits' shows always had a feeling of intimacy as he regaled his audience with stories, jokes and the sort of songs Ilse Lundt would have found herself humming along to Dooley Wilson's piano at Rick's Café in *Casablanca*. Wherever the show though, and whatever the occasion, Tom Waits would always find the time to talk about his favourite subject – shoes.

A short digression: 'Shoes And Their Place In The Tom Waits Canon': While scathing about his songwriting, Waits has expressed an admiration and even affection for the shoes of Neil Young. On his first arrival in England Waits was quick to point out that what the English call winkle-pickers he knew as 'Puerto Rican fence-climbers' or 'ratstickers'. It is also interesting to recall that the artist in question alleges that he was first signed up by Herb Cohen on the strength of his shoes and even claims to have moved to New York because it was "a great town for shoes." Waits also has a novel theory concerning the fluctuating quality of popular music and what you wear on your feet, as he expounded to Gavin Martin: "I think it's a good time for music when it's a good time for shoes. You look in the shoe store and you see them trimmed down with the points just so – they thrill me, really." Waits also confided to Fred Dellar: "Muckalucks are carpet slippers ... Stacey Adams once were a very prestigious shoe ... Staceys stayed ahead of current affairs and were considered extremely hip," viz. 'Tom Traubert's Blues'.

By the time of their respective second albums, Waits and Springsteen were still neck and neck and strangely enough Springsteen's song 'Wild Billy's Circus Story' from 'The Wild, The Innocent And The E. Street Shuffle' sounds uncannily like a Waits song of the period. Both men had an individual songwriting style quite at odds with the prevalent rock mood. Springsteen's fiery brand of rock revivalism echoed the first chill thrill of fifties rock 'n' roll, while Waits was at a whole other ball game, pitching for non-rock influences like Gershwin, Shearing and Sinatra: "I may be a little sentimental, but I'm not nostalgic," he said at this time.

31

He was trying to translate the hard-nosed prose of Nelson Algren into song, to capture the hard-luck stories which walked the streets of concrete canyons. Waits managed to elucidate the urban nightmare, but like the wispy smoke curling from his ever-present cigarette, he was also busy chasing dreams. Above all, Waits was aiming to convey some sort of truth in his songs; the truth that could be found by the side of the railroad track in the small mid-West towns that were really "nothing but a wide spot in the road"; the truth that was found at the bottom of a bottle at closing time.

Waits' caustic love songs were already attracting some attention for their ability to convey very real emotions in a tight and well disciplined song format, but he shucked any real poetic abilities. Asked once whether he was primarily a poet or a singer, Waits deadpanned "I'm a Methodist"; (asked later "are you prolific?" he replied "Well, I was raised a Catholic ..."). He attempted to explain this wariness to *NME*'s Todd Everett in

1975: "Poetry is a very dangerous word ... Most people when they hear the word 'poetry' think of being chained to a school desk memorising 'Ode On A Grecian Urn'. When somebody says that they're going to read me a poem, I can think of any number of things that I'd rather be doing!"

For all this modesty, Waits' experiences on the road were developing into a leathery kind of poetry; hard and shiny, the songs on his second album were more than hard reportage, if Waits wouldn't think it a mortal sin, you could call them poems.

'The Heart Of Saturday Night' marks Tom Waits' authentic début, here are all the hallmarks which would later be associated with his inimitable style. Songs which positively ached with love and loss; jazz arrangements at one with his fifties fondness; lyrics which were alternately pathetic and dryly humorous. This was the album which loudly proclaimed a new talent. This second album also marked the beginning of Waits' partnership with Bones Howe, who would oversee all his albums until 1980. Howe had a notable jazz background, but his mainstream success had been with the glossily acceptable 5th Dimension in the late sixties.

The title track is a classic, with a melody as steady as the Oldsmobile of which Waits sings. In a few scant lines, he manages to convey the freedom and anticipation that Saturday night offers to everyone, everywhere. Waits knows that it 'makes it kind of special, down to the core, 'cause you're dreaming of them Saturdays that came before.' The cycle concludes with the bitter dawn of the album's final track, 'Ghosts Of Saturday Night'. Here is Edward Hopper's painting 'Nighthawks' brought to life, the weary waitress 'Irene', 'with Maxwell House eyes and ... scrambled yellow hair' while Waits salvages 'the last bent butt from a package of Kents.'

These are songs to be heard as you filch the last black dregs from a cup of cold coffee as the dawn dredges up over a row of tenements and the juke-box plays 'Stand By Your Man' for the last time. Whatever warmth the diner offered has dissipated, so it's time to curl up your collar and drift back out on to the city's mean streets where a man must walk alone.

LFI

Peter Anderson

This piano has been drinking *Barry Plummer*

With Rickie Lee Jones backstage at London's Dominion Theatre *Adrian Boot*

London, 1981   *Barry Plummer*

Peter Anderson

LFI

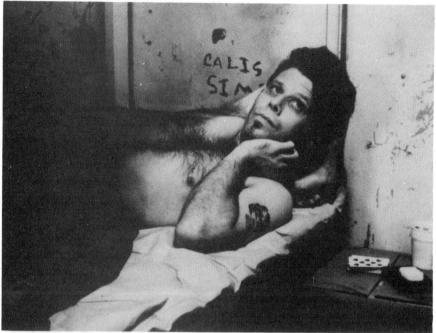

Down By Law 1986   *National Film Archive London*

With Gregory Hines (left) in The Cotton Club 1984   *National Film Archive London*

'Shiver Me Timbers' is a grand song in the American tradition of
exploration; Waits mentions Jack London's *Martin Eden* and Melville's
maritime masterpiece *Moby Dick* as he bids farewell to family and friends
– anything that smacks of attachment – so he can 'skip like a stone' over
untramelled oceans where 'the clouds are like headlines on a new front-
page sky.'

By contrast, the scat-sung 'Diamonds On My Windshield' is driven by a
tautly plucked stand-up bass as Waits barrels down the road on a night
that's 'colder than a well-digger's ass.' The wistful 'San Diego Serenade'
has Waits only appreciating that all his best memories are gone, and sadly
reflecting in the knowledge that it's too late to go back and reclaim them.

Elsewhere on the album, Waits is a dog out in the rain, prowling the
city streets, sticking his nose in other people's business and getting a kick
for his troubles. He's the observer in the back of a yellow cab, casting an
eye out the window at the buildings flashing by. He's the guy leaving the
bar, hat askew, finding an excuse to go back and look for a watch he
thought he'd left there.

The voice is huskier, the presentation less nervous. Waits has every
right to sound more confident; while not claiming for 'The Heart Of
Saturday Night' that much maligned term 'concept album', the songs on it
do have a striking thematic unity. The tracks work together to convey all
the joy and exultation, sorrow and sadness, which make up the moments
you will savour for the rest of the week while you're stuck in your dead-
end job on dead-end street. At least Saturday night lets you celebrate in a
way that is expressly yours. Behind Tom Waits' Saturday night meditation
can be heard the echoes of all those other Saturday nights, of Sam Cooke
and The Drifters, whether it's just 'Another Saturday Night' or 'Saturday
Night At The Movies'.

Already the care Waits lavishes on his writing, the attention he pays to
detailed observation, was becoming apparent. Sitting slumped in the
corner of the diner, unnoticed, but plainly noticing, like he told me ...
"Keeping your anonymity is important as a writer, so that you can go
anywhere, any part of town, sit in a corner. Anytime you're swimming
around in the American public, 'Well people just get uglier, and I have no

sense of time', you know? ... The Devil's Dictionary described being famous as 'conspicuously miserable'!"

Waits' obvious strength as a songwriter included stabs at unorthodox rhyme and observational vignette, but what really kept him apart from the rest of the gang, kept him on the edge, was his fascination with the dark underbelly of American society. While The Eagles could confidently sing of having 'seven women' on their mind, Waits was more interested in the sad hooker and the rising cost of prophylactics. While Neil Young was cautioning of 'Mother Nature on the run in the 1970s', Tom Waits was fidgeting with a Zippo and focusing on a bum to whom home was a cardboard condominium.

Waits was scathing about the sheen that other rock songwriters attached to their work, he let rip to John Platt in 1977: "I can't stand writers that just varnish something and then put it out. I like to know that there was gum under the table ... How many cigarettes were in the ashtray, little things like that. You have to be a little bit of a private investigator to be a good songwriter. 'I rode through the desert on a horse with no name' ... how about 'I rode through the desert on a horse with no legs', that I can see ... 'I almost cut my hair', so what? ... I've tried to get a little closer to the bone because I want to know what really happened. I'd rather have some guy tell me in a song that a drug store was closed and he couldn't get any rubbers, than to tell me that 'The paths of their lives have crossed into the seed of the universe.' That's a lot of cosmic debris ... Maybe you can go broke on underestimating the collective taste or attention span of the American public. I mean, there's a sucker born every minute, and some of them have a lot of money and they spent it on 'A Horse With No Name' ...

"Neil Young is another one who is embarrassing for displaying a third grade mentality. 'Old man take a look at my life' – that's real good – 'it's a lot like yours' – that's great! If he'd come up with that in a bar and not had a pen, it would have been lost to the world. So I'm glad there are always lots of ink and pens and paper around because the man's so gifted."

Between bouts at the Tropicana, Waits was on the road regularly throughout the seventies, and his image and reputation preceded him.

Fans prowled into smoky dives to witness a drunken bum at a piano, a sibilant raconteur with a line in smartass repartee. Waits was living the part off-stage too, but all of those experiences were used, nothing was wasted. Close and brief encounters, exotic images and downbeat language all found themselves swirling beneath the umbrella in Tom Waits' cocktail.

Waits was shortlisted by director Hal Ashby for the starring role in his Woody Guthrie biopic *Bound For Glory*, but mind you, so was every mid-seventies singer-songwriter, including Tim Hardin, Bob Dylan, Tim Buckley and Woody's son Arlo. In typical film style though, the role eventually went to non-singer David Carradine.

To capitalise on Waits' growing reputation by capturing his live performance on vinyl seemed like an astute move, but both critically and commercially, the double live set 'Nighthawks At The Diner' was a disaster. Detractors saw Waits enshrined as The Great Pretender, a pseudo-Beat unworthy of shining Kerouac's boots, and even the fans found this sprawling collection of jazz-style raps better suited to the printed page or nightclub stage. This was where Waits and Springsteen finally went their separate ways, while Waits staggered through the sprawling and unwieldy 'Nighthawks', Bruce's third album was a hot little number called 'Born To Run'.

43

Waits was just trying too hard, determined to prove that he'd travelled as far as Kerouac, and lived as hard as Woody Guthrie; he certainly looked the part, sounded it too – the warm-voiced balladeer of two years previous was little more than a memory, his vocal chords now shot by too many cigarettes. Waits tosses gags and one-liners to the baying crowd like Christians to hungry lions: "I'm so goddam horny the crack o'dawn had better watch out around me"; "Plant you now, dig you later"; "Make like a hockey player and get the puck outta here!" But it's all a bit too laboured, just a mite contrived.

Strangely, Waits' best performance on the album is the set's only cover: Tommy Faile's 'Big Joe And Phantom 309', a variation on 'The Vanishing Hitchhiker', that most persistent of all American folk myths. The song was originally a big C&W hit for Red Sovine in 1967, Sovine also enjoyed a posthumous hit in 1981 with the indescribably gloopy 'Teddy Bear'.

The songs read better than they sound. 'Nighthawk Postcards' is full of lycanthropic detail: 'The El train ... tumbling across the trestles, and it sounded like the ghost of Gene Krupa ... and the whispering brushes of wet radials on wet pavement', with Waits well in character 'using parking meters as walking sticks on the inebriated stroll with my eyelids propped open at half-mast'; or the asthmatic riffs as you quit a bar in 'Putnam County' 'weavin' home, leaving the little joint winking in the dark, warm narcotic American night beneath a pin-cushion sky and it's home to toast and honey ...'

Waits' constituents were clearly identified on 'Eggs And Sausage': 'nighthawks at the diner ... strangers around the coffee urn ... gypsy hacks, insomniacs ...' His was a black and white world, populated by the sort of people Diane Arbus used to photograph, but Waits had nothing but sympathy for his characters, and in his hands their perceived failures attained some sort of spiritual victory.

A good live Tom Waits album would greatly have consolidated his appeal; for audiences weaned on remote, non-verbal superstars, Waits was the perfect antidote. Endlessly chatty, undeniably witty, he cut a compelling figure on-stage. Unfortunately 'Nighthawks' isn't that perfect souvenir. As double live albums go, it's got a long way to go to match Van Morrison's 'It's Too Late To Stop Now', although there are plenty more laughs than Crosby, Stills, Nash And Young's 'Four Way Street'!

With the release of 'Nighthawks At The Diner', Waits took time out to reflect on his position: "Right now I consider myself an unemployed gas station attendant. I'm a legend in my own mind, a kind of rumour in my own time, a tumour on my own mind. I'm not on the verge of national prominence or anything."

Waits' "emotional weather report" had him down but not out, bloody but unbowed. Through the permanent haze of cigarette smoke, in a suit that looked like it had been slept in by the entire Off-Broadway cast of *Waiting For Godot*, skeletal hands waving through the spotlit dark and all the time, weaving his tales in a voice like a Cadillac with a snapped

44

exhaust, Waits was gaining a reputation. The Big Time still beckoned, but our boy was on his way, albeit slowly: "I've never met anyone who made it with a chick because they owned a Tom Waits album. I've got all three and it's never helped me!"

46

CHAPTER THREE

'And no one speaks English and everything's broken ...'
'Tom Traubert's Blues', Tom Waits, 1976.

Tom Waits left America behind for the first time in 1976. Aged 26, Waits had heard rumours of a world beyond the Santa Monica Boulevard, and went out to look for it.

Appropriately Waits made his British début at Ronnie Scott's Club in Soho, which has been immortalised by its patron with the words "This place reminds me of home – filthy, and full of strangers." Soho was London's Bohemia, the smudge of vermilion lipstick on the grey face of the capital. The strip shows, luridly enticing on the outside, inside about as erotic as a WI Bring and Buy, the drinking clubs, the patisseries and bistros of old Soho ... Waits loved it.

Rock music was undergoing its most seismographic change of the decade, punk's assault and battery left grizzled sixties survivors baffled as the Young Turks went on search and destroy missions for fresh targets. Tom Waits shuffled a Stacey and stayed outside the maelstrom.

Waits was a godsend to journalists. For too long during the seventies, rock stars had used interviews as platforms for their own half-baked philosophies, and watched smugly as endless columns of print were filled with their egocentric ramblings. Tom Waits gave great copy, he used interviews as a springboard for ideas that he'd then incorporate in his act, any hapless journalist hoping for anything approximating to the 'truth' was bound to come away disappointed, but most ended up with enough quotes to fill a dictionary. Using libation as libido, Waits rambled through the thesaurus, dropped names like a raging bull in a glass factory and emerged blinking at the daylight.

Waits was only too happy to live out the image of the drunken bum, cigarette ash flying as he wheezed through a routine fuelled by an endless supply of booze. John Platt recalls Waits spending 45 minutes building up an unrepeatable joke about Hank Snow and June Carter over countless drinks, while Peter O'Brien remembers trailing after Waits through a series of Soho pubs, caught up in the wake of a freewheeling 'interview'. "Don't go to the Compton drive-in on a Saturday night and announce over the loudspeaker that you are responsible for the death of Malcolm X. If you go to the Tropicana Hotel, watch out for Chuck E. Weiss, he'll sell you a rat's asshole for a wedding ring ... I'm afraid I'm gonna be walking along someday in Los Angeles and drop into a manhole, and down there's gonna be 500 unemployed bossa nova musicians and they're gonna 'Girl From Ipanema' me to death ... The only thing I hate is bluegrass played poorly. I guess the only thing I hate more than that is bluegrass played well."

English writers were fascinated by the very idea of the Beat culture which Waits seemed to embody; post-war Baby Boomers only got the freedom which *On The Road* had promised second-hand. Meandering down a B-road in a Morris Minor to Paignton somehow lacked the urgency of cruising over the Mexican border to a Tijuana brothel in a '56 Chevy. The heady brew offered by Waits' icons were all too rarely tasted in the stuffy Britain of the late fifties and early sixties – Lenny Bruce had actually been deported by the Home Secretary following his only appearance at

The Establishment Club in Soho, when he insinuated that Prince Charles was really a 40-year-old midget.

Waits breezed in exuding the very essence of American hip. At the same time that Frampton Came Alive, Tom Waits slumped in half-dead. His Ronnie's début was as much mouth as music: "I've been riding on the crest of a slump lately," he confided to the crowd. "I've played a place where the average age was deceased." Barry Manilow this wasn't. Between insults, Waits settled down to play some meditative piano and make music that wasn't out of place at Ronnie's, but was a long way from the pop charts. Aptly, the NME review of his London début referred to him as 'Tom Wits'.

While enjoying his stint at Ronnie's, Waits did admit that "most nightclubs are more concerned with serving lager than putting a spotlight on you" – like the actor who, playing a church hall in Scotland, instructed the stage manager, "I'd like a single spot on me when I make my entrance, backlit for the soliloquy then full flood for the finale" only to be met with the deflating question "You want the switch up or down?"

49

Quitting England's green and pleasant shores, Waits toured round Finland, Norway, Holland and Germany, an experience which provided the basis for one of his finest ever songs, 'Tom Traubert's Blues'. Indeed, many of the experiences from that first European tour found their way onto Waits' next album; 'The Piano Has Been Drinking (An Evening With Pete King)' referred to the co-owner of Ronnie Scott's Club, while 'Tom Traubert's' subtitle had Waits 'Four Sheets To The Wind In Copenhagen'.

During his time in Soho, Waits gave some very good advice when he cautioned us to "Watch out for 16-year-old girls wearing bell bottoms who are running away from home and have a lot of Blue Oyster Cult records under their arm." But the best was yet to come; on the point of returning home he allowed his public a rare and revealing insight into his craft: "I'm going back to Los Angeles to get drunk as a skunk and stay that way for three days, then I'm going right into the studio."

'Small Change' was recorded in a five-day blitz in July 1976, and remains one of Waits' best ever albums. It was the album which proved beyond doubt that Tom Waits was far more than a hangover from the fifties, that he could stand independently as a major songwriter of the seventies. The album has wit, pathos, pith and vinegar. It was the quality and individuality of Waits' work on this album which finally convinced me that he was more than just a passing novelty; alongside the quintessence of Waits which was distilled on 'Small Change', the accusation of plagiarist could simply no longer stand up.

Like anyone with a 'personal tendency' towards singer-songwriters, I'd been waiting for the 'new Dylan' of the seventies. As it happened, the old one wasn't doing so bad by then – the excoriating 'Blood On The Tracks' in 1974 showed that, as he entered his thirties, Dylan could still tell a story like no one else in rock; 1975's 'Desire' displayed all the diversity which boded well for the rest of the decade, and the gipsy caravan of the Rolling Thunder Review found Dylan reaching a new frontier. But Rolling Thunder never made it across the Atlantic, and besides, shouldn't there be someone *of* the seventies *for* the seventies?

50

I had been unimpressed by the hype surrounding Springsteen's make or break third album 'Born To Run', the furore struck me as born of desperation, the rock establishment frantically searching for someone, anyone, to handle the Dylan mantle. Death had taken Gram Parsons and Tim Buckley, Rita Coolidge had got Kris Kristofferson, and the 'new Dylans' like John Prine, Steve Forbert, Loudon Wainwright and Steve Goodman just didn't pack the necessary punch.

Rock music, which had promised so much at the end of the sixties, was now reneging on the deal. Like so many others who had been lured along for the ride, I felt betrayed by the mid-seventies. Instead of concentrating on getting a real education, I really thought I had found a viable alternative in the rock culture, and that singer-songwriters could take me the necessary steps ahead. Well, that idea went right up the funnel pretty smart.

What I found in 'Small Change' was authenticity; Waits sounded like he knew what he was singing about, there was a veracity to those songs. It wasn't that he glorified bums or elevated derelicts into venerated rebels, rather that he documented their situation and dreams with an honesty and with compassion. Much as he'd squirm at the prospect, Waits did it all with a poet's eye. Acutely, touchingly, he drew us into his world, a kind of urban Hades, songs which evoked the rain-soaked streets of *Taxi Driver*. Lyrically punching out, recounting his tales in a voice that sounded like he gargled with gravel before his morning hair of the dog.

It wasn't all sturm and drang, that's what ultimately sold me on 'Small Change'; too often I'd made the mistake of wallowing in the company of outsiders on record, as if it was only right down at the bottom of the barrel that the truth could be found. Waits sounded like he was on first-name terms with those types, but he also, mercifully, had a sense of humour, which is what made the album so resilient and refreshing.

It wasn't just that rock had lost direction in the mid-seventies, I was also bored rigid by the music's over-earnest pomposity. Parallel to Dylan's 'finger-pointing' songs had been his impish wit, and in the sixties for every 'Like A Rolling Stone' there had been a 'Tombstone Blues'. Frank Zappa had cast a caustic eye over the hippies on 'We're Only In It For The Money' and the late-lamented Bonzo Dog Band had satirically shafted rock behemoths with 'Can Blue Men Sing The Whites?' and the classic 'Canyons Of Your Mind': 'Each time I hear your name, oh, how it hurts, in the wardrobe of my soul, in the section labelled shirts!'

As well as the anger of its intentions, punk did have the residual benefit of spiky humour, usually taking the form of fondly loved sixties songs ('Help', 'Nights In White Satin') thrashed with amphetamine energy. But punk aside, there had been precious little to laugh at in rock since those halcyon days, unless of course you include solo albums by David Crosby and Graham Nash.

Waits certainly seemed like the sort of chap who'd enjoy a good joke, and he was able to remember and jot down all those snappy one-liners and put-downs you'd forgotten in the pub the night before. Once Tom Waits had brought his hangover into focus, I reckoned there was a weighty talent to be considered, so 'Small Change' was doubly welcome. I was convinced that now Waits had sifted through the small change in his pockets, he'd strike the mother lode in his suit sometime soon.

We knew now that the preceding three albums had simply been trailers for the main feature. The majestic opening track 'Tom Traubert's

Blues' is a distillation of Waits' greatness, as the foghorn voice booms out, he effortlessly evokes urban despair and big city isolation without ever sounding maudlin. He even managed to incorporate the chorus of 'Waltzing Matilda' into the 1976 song: "'Waltzing Matilda' was written in about 1903. I think the gals who wrote it are still around. But I didn't have any trouble. It goes over real well in England," Waits told Bill Flanagan in 1987. "'Waltzing Matilda' is very sentimental over there because it's about the English going off, disappearing from the homeland. 'Matilda' is a backpack. When you're 'waltzing Matilda' you're on the road. You're not with your girlfriend, you're on the bum. For me, I was in Europe for the first time and I felt like a soldier far away from home and drunk on the corner with no money, lost. I had a hotel key and I didn't know where I was. That kind of feeling."

In his book *The Romance Of Song* Henry Lawson tells us in all innocence: "Travelling with swag in Australia is variously and picturesquely described as 'humping bluey', 'walking Matilda', 'humping Matilda', 'humping your drum', 'being on the wallaby' ..."

'Waltzing Matilda' has also been used to great effect in later years, by one of Waits' favourite bands The Pogues, on their version of Eric Bogle's magnificent 'The Band Played Waltzing Matilda', still one of the most damning and poignant anti-war songs ever written.

As for the title track 'Small Change (Got Rained On With His Own .38)', Waits admitted: "I even kinda impressed myself with that one" before going on to cite the song's source as the film *Pete Kelly's Blues* (starring *Dragnet*'s Jack Webb) and allowing that his song also contained elements of Mickey Spillane, Perry Mason, Damon Runyon and Nelson Algren.

The song is a blinding tour-de-force, an odyssey into the nightmare of film noir. You can visualise John Garfield with the racing paper sticking out of his back pocket slumped in his own blood, staining the linoleum by the juke-box while the cops (Edmund O'Brien and William Bendix) 'are cracking jokes about some whorehouse in Seattle.' Outside in the yellow bargain store night-light 'the naked mannequins with their Cheshire grins' stand silent as a distant siren splits the night, like some great wounded creature limping off home to die. 'Small Change' is just another statistic that night.

When we met, Waits spoke to me at length of his fondness for New Orleans "the bosom of American music," and nowhere is that affection more apparent than on the evocative 'I Wish I Was In New Orleans': listening 'to that tenor saxophone callin' me home, and I can hear the band begin 'When The Saints Go Marching In'.' New Orleans, 'The Big Easy', where, Kerouac wrote, the air "was so sweet ... it seemed to come in soft bandannas." That most un-American of American cities, nuzzling next to the muddy Mississippi, on which the riverboat gamblers plied their trade as the chugging wheels bore them past the twilit ante-bellum mansions. New Orleans' Preservation Hall, the home of jazz, where the sign above the tiny stage reads 'Requests, $5.00; 'The Saints', $10!''

The album's laconic humour abounds: 'The Piano Has Been Drinking' describes the sort of purgatory we all visit every once in a while, where you can't find your waitress 'even with a geiger counter', you're conversing with someone who has 'the IQ of a fence-post' and the bouncer 'looks like a Sumo wrestler.' 'Step Right Up' discusses the universal panacea: 'It' 'entertains relatives ... turns you into a nine-year-old Hindu boy ... gives you an erection and wins the election' before winding up with the sage advice 'the large print giveth, and the small print taketh away.' 'Jitterbug Boy' has Waits as ubiquitous show-off, the man who slept with Marilyn Monroe, punched out Rocky Marciano, got slewed with Satchmo and shot pool with Minnesota Fats. While the wisecracking 'One That Got Away' has the 'shroud tailor measuring for a deep six holiday.'

53

The downside of Waits' songs is the dark landscape of the American dream, as on 'Bad Liver And A Broken Heart' where 'the moon ain't romantic, it's intimidating as hell' and 'Small Change''s 'the dreams aren't broken down here, they're walking with a limp.' That's the territory Tom Waits was staking out for himself: where all the loners congregate on windswept street corners, or find themselves, condemned to life, in small windswept Texas towns where the entire population turns out to watch the traffic lights change. This is the cast of 'Small Change', the dreamers whose dreams have been battered on the anvil of greed. Waits sympathises with the losers, with the ones that got away, but also with those forced to stay behind; all those who never get a slice of the cake but are just left fingering the packaging.

Even the cover of 'Small Change' had Waits comfortably at home, bleary-eyed in a stripper's dressing room, like Woody Allen in *What's New Pussycat*. "What do you do?" asks Peter O'Toole. "I help the strippers dress and undress," says Woody. "What's the pay like?" "$20 a week." "That's not much." "I know but it's all I can afford." Waits was the kind of buy Central Casting would send round when anyone rang up for a downbeat, a bum. He cast his eye on the sleazy side of the street, a chronicler for the down and outs, but he did it with compassion, even empathised with the characters, rather than viewing them as if through a microscope with distaste.

Waits went back on the road in the States, but now began to recognise its limitations: "The uncontrollable urge to play Iowa has finally left me." He was willing to play the game by the rules, though; if you made a new album, you went out on the road to promote it. You also found yourself confronting DJs and chat show hosts who'd been hoping for Rod Stewart. They sure as hell didn't know what to make of the guy who staggered in, plumped himself down by a piano and growled through a series of songs about pimps, pasties and a G-string. In the interview book, singer-songwriters who played the piano were from the same mould as Elton John, Barry Manilow, Randy Newman and Billy Joel; one look at Tom Waits though and chat show hosts fastened their seat belts for a bumpy night.

On the *Fernwood Tonight* TV show in 1977, for example, Waits managed to convince the baffled hosts that the only reason he was there was because his touring van had broken down on the way to somewhere else where he'd far rather be. He even succeeded in borrowing $20 off one baffled interviewer ("But I had to leave the four-year-old as collateral"). Neatly sidestepping inquiries about his background ("I got an apartment on the corner of Bedlam and Squalor") Waits philosophised "I've always maintained that reality is for people who can't face drugs" before moving on to music: "Got a new song, 'Breakfast In Jail', it's actually a dance number 'Do The Breakfast In Jail'!" and claiming that his new album was an opus entitled 'Music To Seduce A Divorced Waitress By'.

Between stints on the road, it was back to his $9 a night room at the Tropicana, with his piano in the kitchen, and where his girlfriend Rickie Lee Jones also lived. Jones was born in 1955, and moved to LA in 1973 where she worked as a waitress before falling in with a 'Bohemian' crowd that included Waits and Chuck E. Weiss, whom she commemorated on her 1979 hit 'Chuck E's In Love'. Weiss also co-wrote one track on Waits' 'Nighthawks' and is name-checked on 'Jitterbug Boy' and 'I Wish I Was In New Orleans'.

Waits and Jones were an 'item' for some years, she is featured on the sleeve of his 'Blue Valentine' and his otherwise unavailable 'Rainbow Sleeves' is included on her mini-album 'Girl At Her Volcano' (the song also appeared in 1983 on the soundtrack of Martin Scorsese's marvellous, underrated film *King Of Comedy*.) Despite her own songwriting abilities and a passing resemblance to the young Kathleen Turner, Jones' career faltered irrevocably in the eighties, as did her relationship with Waits. She once confided to journalist Timothy White that the relationship was doomed because what Tom really wanted was to live in a little bungalow with a bunch of screaming kids and spend Saturday nights at the drive-in.

55

The real danger was that instead of such cosy domesticity, Waits was living the lifestyle he portrayed in his songs and his stage show; "An inebriated good evening to you all" wasn't just a snappy opening line, during the rigorous years of touring throughout the seventies, Tom Waits' view of life was telescoped through the bottom of a bottle. It was all a part of the 'image', the sloshed poet, the sozzled raconteur, the low-life 'professional eavesdropper'; but it all took its toll. Most interviews with Waits at that time were conducted in the convivial surroundings of a bar, with the subject suitably soused. Waits had successfully invented a character, and now found himself honour-bound to live it to the hilt.

There were of course notable precedents: Brendan Behan and Dylan Thomas who in his cups once remarked "Somebody's boring me – I think it's me." In interview, Waits was still great value, his interviews as much a performance as the paid gigs, but with the steady flow of liquor, Waits began to display all the hallmarks of the classic drunk. "Had an Indian meal last night, the food was so bad I didn't know whether to eat it or drive it home," he told Mike Flood Page three times in two hours in 1976.

Cynics saw Waits as a sham, the kind of drunk you avoided in a bar because you knew he'd buttonhole you and start getting maudlin about a waitress he knew who looked just like Lana Turner. They resented his wholesale hijacking of the Beat myth, his irritating reverence for obscure jazzers and the mouth permanently in overdrive. As if to convince the doubters of his authenticity, Waits ensured his voice got more ragged, pulled onboard a brewery for company, and let rip.

He did have his fans though. Devotees who welcomed Waits' breath of stale air revelled in his iconoclastic commentary and relished his after hours view of life. Waits fans delighted in his street credentials. When Tom Waits sang about 'The One That Got Away' they relished the fact that he'd been down there at the bottom; not for Waits a *Reader's Digest* view of life in the bargain bin, Tom had been there and drunk the sourmash.

Waits was becoming bitter at the absence of commercial success which he felt 'Small Change' deserved: "I don't get played on the radio. Ever. Marcel Marceau gets more airplay than I do!" The musical climate in 1977 wasn't particularly favourable to a character like Tom Waits. It was a case of being caught between two extremes, the cosy AOR of Fleetwood Mac and The Eagles on the one hand or the nihilistic fervour of The Sex Pistols on the other. Somewhere off on an inebriated tangent was Tom Waits' sleazy style of lowlife jazz. Following the critical triumph of 'Small Change', Waits was gaining plaudits, but he'd deliberately talked his way out of any convenient pigeonhole. A voice like his didn't, couldn't, make for easy listening.

'Foreign Affairs' wasn't as coherent an album as its predecessor, although it did contain two classic Waits edge of darkness workouts on 'Potter's Field' and 'Burma Shave', as well as 'I Never Talk To Strangers', the duet with Bette Midler which first alerted director Francis Ford Coppola to Waits' work.

Much of the album resulted from the aftermath of Waits' European tour, and the heightened awareness of his own country it had imbued in him. 'Jack And Neal' was Waits' long overdue vinyl testimony to the influence of Kerouac and Cassady, while 'Muriel' and 'A Sight For Sore Eyes' were beautiful bittersweet love songs with some of Waits' most enticing melodies.

At the core of the album though are the two lengthy narrative pieces. 'Potter's Field' came at you 'from the edge of a maniac's dream,' a dark odyssey of betrayal and misplaced trust, populated by hoods who'd sell their mother 'if it was whiskey that they paid.' 'Burma Shave' was inspired by Nick Ray's 1947 film *They Live By Night* starring Farley Granger who is mentioned in the song. It's an edgy, restless piece, dealt from the same deck as James M. Cain's *The Postman Always Rings Twice*. In Waits' song, you can visualise the same small, dead town, as the trucks thunder past on the highway, and 'everybody's got one foot in the grave.' In that graveyard, the very idea of somewhere like 'Burma Shave' is intoxicating; it becomes a Shangri La, beckoning to those who are condemned to living death in the suffocatingly small backwater. You can sense the elation of escape as you 'count the grain elevators in the rear view mirror,' each one leaving Marysville further behind.

57

It was the kind of place that Malcolm Muggeridge, of all people, wrote about in 1958: "Driving at night into the town of Athens, Ohio (pop.3450) four bright coloured signs stood out in the darkness – 'Gas', 'Drugs', 'Beauty', 'Food'. Here, I thought, is the ultimate, the logos of our time, presented in sublime simplicity. It was like a vision in which suddenly all the complexity of life is reduced to one single inescapable proposition. These signs could have shone forth as clearly in Athens, Greece, as in Athens, Ohio. All the world loves Lucy."

Waits was slow in following up 'Foreign Affairs', but he wasn't being idle. Keen to shake off the tour-album-tour cycle, Waits cast up as a piano player aptly named Mumbles in one of Sylvester Stallone's post-Rocky movies, 1978's *Paradise Alley*. Before Stallone cast himself as America's national conscience, thuggish John Rambo, and before Rocky Balboa became a right-wing flag-waver, Stallone was willing to take risks. Rocky's first adventure was an upbeat movie about a punch-drunk no-hoper which found the Italian Stallion favourably compared to a young Brando.

Paradise Alley was a competent attempt at recreating Warner Brothers' 'Hell's Kitchen' New York dramas of the forties. Waits had a cough and a spit as a bar room pianist, and the film also featured an early appearance from Anne Archer, later to find fame as the put-upon wife in *Fatal Attraction*. Waits later admitted he undertook the Stallone movie simply for the money, but it was valuable experience and whetted his appetite for more movie work.

Another project between albums was the screenplay *Why Is The Dream So Much Sweeter Than The Taste?*, which was "about a used-car salesman and a racetrack announcer who change identities." Written in collaboration with Paul Hampton, a colleague of songwriter Burt Bacharach, the script had originally been developed by Waits from his own idea, an imaginatively titled piece 'Used Carlotta'. Sadly the script was to remain unrealised, although elements of it did later find their way into 'Christmas Card From A Hooker In Minneapolis': 'I wish I had all the money we used to spend on dope, I'd buy a used car lot and I wouldn't sell any of 'em, I'd just drive a different car every day, depending on how I feel.' Waits also expanded the car lot theme in 'One From The Heart' and one of the film's most touching scenes has Frederic Forrest conducting an orchestra of wrecked cars with a dipstick.

Another tantalising project of that time was initiated when Waits found himself approached by artist Guy Peellaert – renowned for his illustrated *Rock Dreams* – and asked to supply the prose to accompany Peellaert's drawings of Las Vegas personalities: Liberace, Frank Sinatra, Judy Garland, Howard Hughes etc. For various logistical reasons, the Waits and Peellaert book never came to fruition, and it was Michael Herr, author of *Dispatches*, the best ever book about Vietnam, who supplied the text for Peellaert's collection of drawings called *The Big Room*, which was eventually published in 1986.

It was around this time that Waits grew seriously disillusioned with the music industry, and his seemingly negligible role in it. Three years later, looking back on his situation Waits told me: "I was totally disenchanted with the music business. I moved to New York and was seriously considering other possible career alternatives. The whole Modus

58

Operandi," he continued, making it sound like a particularly noxious branch of the Cosa Nostra, "of sitting down and writing and making an album, going out on the road with a band. Away for three months, come back with high blood pressure, a drinking problem, tuberculosis, a warped sense of humour. It just became predictable."

Back in the studio in the summer of 1978 that predictability was manifest. 'Blue Valentine' was Waits' fifth studio album and although it showed him moving away from the piano towards electric guitar, for the first time I had the feeling that I'd been here before. 'Romeo Is Bleeding' to my ears sounded like a pale re-run of 'Small Change' and for all his efforts not even Waits can redeem 'Blue Valentines' from sounding like a Tom Waits parody.

The album opens with Waits' assault and battery on 'Somewhere' from *West Side Story*. Waits reasoned that no one since P. J. Proby had covered the song properly so he aimed to restore the balance. The rest of the album was a stagger through familiar Waits territory, where his venom was reserved for those who destroyed the sanctity of dreams. At its best, the album was a confident reclamation of familiar Waits territory, for sure there weren't many others writing songs with titles like 'Christmas Card From A Hooker In Minneapolis' or 'A Sweet Little Bullet From A Pretty Little Gun'.

The album's best song, 'Christmas Card From A Hooker In Minneapolis' is a heartbreaking open letter, partly truth and partly fiction, recalling a romance bordered by filling stations, Little Anthony And The Imperials' records and used car lots, only to be knocked sideways in the final verse by the realisation that it's just a come-on for some cash. The whole thing was just a sad fabrication, there never was any husband, just someone trying to invent a past that never was. In concert, Waits would frequently preface the song with 'Silent Night', and muster a snatch of Little Anthony's 1964 hit 'Goin' Out Of My Head' for good measure.

Vocally, Waits had mislaid a lot of the gravelly timbre which had so spoilt 'Foreign Affairs', there was no return to the softer pastures of his début, but the rasp was on hold. His writing eye was as sharp as ever: at his best, Waits could weave dreams as successfully as his compadre Bruce

Springsteen, but Waits' dreams had a darker side, he recognised the innate fallibility of his characters, identified with their predicaments and saw their despair. Waits' characters stood stripped of dignity, but with just a whiff of spunk left to punch out and not be ground down. There was little glory in Waits' songs on 'Blue Valentine', on 'Whistling Past The Graveyard', the only glory Waits' eyes have seen is 'the drainin' of the ditch.'

While now renowned for his lowlife chronicles, there was a gentler side to Tom Waits, which can be found on the poignant 'Kentucky Avenue', an autobiographical song which has the composer casting an affectionate glance back at his childhood. In typical Waits fashion this was no soppy, soft focus memoir: 'Kentucky Avenue' concludes with a dream of making it to New Orleans, but only after Waits has freed his heroine from her wheelchair and the braces on her leg.

Waits was allowed plenty of freedom when it came to making albums. From early on Asylum recognised that this boy wasn't going to keep them very busy pressing up platinum albums or shipping out promo singles to Top Forty stations. Even given that freedom, Tom Waits found himself wanting to attack something more substantial as, like a broken music box, the seventies wound to a close.

CHAPTER FOUR

61

Up to his neck in napalm and jungle, marooned in the Philippines with an idea which even looks set to bust its $31 million budget, Francis Ford Coppola realises two things: (1) He is an artist and (2) He is going quietly insane.

Mud, blood and bullets are closer to him than members of his own family. Coppola has fought battles for his films before, but this time it's war. He is the general in charge of an army that's trying to fully convey the gore of war, attempting to achieve the impossible: to communicate 'The horror, the horror.'

Comparisons abound with another Hollywood wonderkid. As the basis for his Vietnam fable, Coppola is using Joseph Conrad's 1902 novel *Heart Of Darkness*; forty years before, another young director, Orson Welles, had intended the Conrad novel as his first film, but instead was forced to fall back on his own imagination and create *Citizen Kane*.

In the Philippines the budget has gone haywire, eating up all Coppola's profits from the phenomenally successful *Godfather* films. Steve McQueen, Al Pacino and Gene Hackman have all turned down roles in Coppola's recreation of Vietnam. Coppola's final choice of star, Martin Sheen, has had a nervous breakdown while on location. At least, reasons the Mephistophelian figure of Coppola, things can't get any worse ... Sheen then suffers a heart attack. During his Wagnerian evocation of a squadron of helicopters napalming a village, Coppola suddenly realises he cannot communicate with the helicopters from the ground ... Then there's the hurricane that is promised and still 'CHARLIE DON'T SURF!'

"*Apocalypse Now* is not a movie. It is not about Vietnam. It is Vietnam," Coppola later admitted. "We were in the jungle; there were too many of us; we had access to too much money, too much equipment. And, little by little, we went insane." From that insanity, something magic emerged. Sheen's quest for the elusive, ethereal Kurtz of Marlon Brando remains one of the cinema's most astonishing odysseys; a journey that begins with the screen erupting in a frighteningly beautiful eruption of napalm and at the very start has Jim Morrison coolly confiding that this is 'The End'.

Despite the fact that the finished film is still the only one to fully capture the madness, scale and ultimate futility of the Vietnam war, *Apocalypse Now* never did the socko Box Office business that was needed to restore Coppola's roller-coaster fortunes. What Francis badly needed next was a quick, quiet, low-key movie to break even and help restore his sanity. But it took three years to realise. It was called *One From The Heart* and yet again it helped Francis Ford Coppola familiarise himself with the term 'bankruptcy'.

Coppola had been Godfather to the 'Movie Brats' (George Lucas, John Milius, Steven Spielberg, Martin Scorsese etc) and was known as a maverick in an industry where conformity is considered safer. Coppola's flair and vision could on occasion be dovetailed with commercial success: he had won an Oscar for his script of George C. Scott's widely acclaimed

Patton, had fashioned a memorable screenplay for the 1974 version of Scott Fitzgerald's *The Great Gatsby* and had patiently nurtured Lucas' *American Graffiti* at a time when no other producer would touch it.

Though by no means the first choice for director, it was also Coppola who had turned Mario Puzo's pot-boiling novel *The Godfather* into not one, but two magnificent films; indeed *The Godfather Part Two* has the distinction of being the only sequel ever to win the Academy Award for 'Best Film'. The two *Godfather* films had made Coppola immensely bankable, now he was in the position to make offers that nobody could refuse. But rather than play safe, Coppola was winging it again.

As far back as 1969, the 30-year-old Coppola had a vision of managing an independent film studio in Hollywood, a studio which would encourage new talent and act as a factory for the best elements of new American cinema; but the dream didn't become a reality until the box office receipts for both *Godfather* films began pouring in and it became obvious that they could bankroll Coppola's vision. Zoetrope (from the Greek, literally meaning 'wheel of life') came into being in 1980 when Coppola purchased the old Hollywood General Studios in Los Angeles for around $7 million.

63

Coppola's choice of name for his new studio suggested the co-operative nature of the venture. In the 19th century, Zoetrope was the name given to a machine which, for the first time, provided the means for seemingly moving pictures to be witnessed simultaneously by a group of people. The cylindrical metal drum had a series of slits around its sides through which viewers could glimpse the illustrations on the strip of paper inside, when rotated the machine gave the impression of motion. The strips of paper were relatively cheap to produce and easy to change, so that people were able to build up their own collections. After a hard day Empire-building, the Victorians liked nothing better than to relax in front of a flickering Zoetrope before settling down to the latest Dickens in easy instalments.

The escalating problems of *Apocalypse Now* which took five years to realise, had seen the mogul marooned in the Philippines in the vortex of a

spiralling budget; now Coppola envisaged his first Zoetrope film as a
safety valve. He needed a project that would let him blow off steam and
help him to forget the madness he had created in the jungle. Coppola
needed to escape the unbearable pressure of his Vietnam epic, but he
needed above all a lightweight, low budget hit and run movie that would
get Zoetrope off the starting blocks.

Coppola recognised something of interest in a script submitted to him
by Armyan Bernstein, a story set in Chicago, and Coppola was drawn into
his "fantasy about romantic love, jealousy and sex." At the back of his
mind Coppola already had various ideas which he was keen to incorporate
into his next film. It was while directing a stage version of Noel Coward's
Private Lives some years earlier that Coppola first became attracted to
the idea of using songs not simply as background music but as a direct
commentary on the characters, their actions and motivations. More
recently, increasingly fascinated by the Japanese Kabuki style of theatre,
Coppola had found himself walking through Tokyo's garish Ginza area and
being reminded irresistibly of Las Vegas: "the last frontier of America." In
his fertile mind, Coppola had already transported Bernstein's double-
handed love story from Chicago to Vegas.

For Coppola, Vegas symbolised many aspects of America. The vacuous
neon Sodom standing isolated in the middle of the Nevada desert. The last
resort, where Howard Hughes holed up in paranoid seclusion, where Elvis
Presley held garish court and where 24 hours a day, the fruit machines
were pumped by avaricious hordes, all hungry for their big slice of the
American Dream. Coppola envisaged Vegas as the ideal background for
his film, which had at its heart a very simple love story: 24 hours in the
lives of one couple over a July 4th weekend, riding an emotional roller-
coaster as they fell in and out of love, drifted apart and then back
together, their every deed lit by the gaudy, glaring Vegas lights.

A complex million dollars worth of state-of-the-art technology
ensured that Coppola could save $2 million on pre-production work – that
was until he decided to build his very own Las Vegas on the Zoetrope lot,

at a cost of nearly $5 million! The principal actors on *One From The Heart* – Frederic Forrest, Nastassia Kinski, Raul Julia and Teri Garr – were already on the Zoetrope roster, and Coppola had a clear idea of how the film's music should be a fully integrated part of the narrative, the songs written in tandem with the script rather than added on as an afterthought. The director spoke enthusiastically of doing away "with all the psychological motivation stuff, and placing people as part of the composition, in which scenery, acting, words, lyrics, colour ... all come together with equal importance."

"*One From The Heart* was the most rewarding experience I've had since I started working," Waits told me while he was on sabbatical from the movie. "Francis is always changing his mind when he gets inside a film, then he eats his way out ... he's a creative maverick who is distrusted by all the cigar-smoking moguls. He keeps morale up, like Orson Welles said, a movie studio is the best train set you could ever want. Coppola keeps a child's wonder at the whole process, even after a business meeting. I was a very undisciplined writer until I began to work with Francis ... the seasons when you're working for a major company aren't necessarily the same seasons which coincide with your own creative development."

Rumours had Coppola considering Van Morrison for the score – Al Stewart may have been touting for work too, his 1981 song 'Here In Angola' included the winning rhyme 'Take another sip of your cola/ You'll be the colonel of the cavalry/ I'll be Francis Ford Coppola.' But Coppola heard the Tom Waits and Bette Midler duet 'I Never Talk To Strangers' and knew he needed to look no further. Midler was also intended as Waits' partner on the film soundtrack but contractual complications saw C&W chanteuse Crystal Gayle hired instead. Waits himself was delighted at being asked to undertake the complexities of film scoring, and spent nearly two years slaving over his contribution to *One From The Heart*.

The importance of *One From The Heart* in Tom Waits' career is not simply that it gave him the opportunity to score a multi-million dollar film, it also marked his coming of age as a writer. Until his full-time

65

involvement with Coppola, Waits had simply supplied songs
spontaneously. For every album, he'd write 20 or so for consideration,
then sift them down to the required 12. By his own admission, most of his
writing owed a healthy debt to the odd aperitif.

One From The Heart was different. He was given a piano in an office
on the Zoetrope lot, and went in every day to collaborate with Coppola on
his songs and their place at the heart of Coppola's film. Waits likened his
writing experiences on the project to being one of the old Brill Building
songwriting stalwarts, but was fulsome in his praise of Coppola and his
admirable determination to follow that dream. The inherent discipline
demanded by film scoring and by Coppola gave Waits a lasting confidence
and imposed some much needed order onto his chaos. It was an
experience for which Waits has good reason to be thankful.

"Coppola is actually the only film director in Hollywood that has a
conscience ... who is selfless in that he sees himself as a conduit and a part
of something much larger. He's concerned with the future of the cinema ...
most of them are egomaniacs and money-grabbing bastards ... He's
concerned with developing not just an acting repertory company but also
... a place where you can have a full emotional curriculum, dealing with
every aspect of the fine arts. Francis is very musical, and one of the
warmest, most open, vulnerable, mad, imaginative people I've ever met.
He gave me an office with a piano, with venetian blinds, wood panelling
and a view of the gas station! And I got up in the morning, shaved, put on a
suit and went to work ...

"Francis was shooting with a PA system on the set. When he's
rehearsing he plays the music and then the actors can listen and grow
accustomed to hearing that melody while they're working on a scene, and
it's like, put together much more like a theatre production than a movie.
And he wants to shoot it in sequence, so you get a real feeling for the story
and you see magic while you're making it, not months later, where people
stand back and say it's great, but it was two years of hell. What he's trying
to do is get everyone to enjoy the process and leave it open for new ideas.

Francis loves somebody to tell him that something's not possible, and he'll make it possible," Waits told Dermot Stokes of *Hot Press*.

Over the years, Waits' fondness for Coppola has not diminished, despite the claustrophobia of film work and the endless, inevitable time-wasting it entails: "I don't think there's anyone quite like Francis. He's a con-man and a carney and a little dictator and an exotic bird, a schoolteacher, ballerina, pimp, a clown and a buffoon and a president and a trash collector. He makes good spaghetti ... very Italian. Francis Ford Mussolini. I love him dearly."

Coppola was in turn enchanted by Waits' work, calling him "the prince of melancholy." In addition to his music for the film, Waits can be glimpsed on screen near the beginning of *One From The Heart* as a trumpet player, and sensing his disenchantment with 'just' music, Coppola was also to employ Waits' talents as an actor in his three subsequent films.

67

Following the successful integration of Paul Simon's songs in *The Graduate* in 1967, Hollywood had woken up to the immense box office potential of incorporating rock music on the soundtracks of their films; Coppola himself had used songs by The Lovin' Spoonful in his first major directorial project, *You're A Big Boy Now*, in the same year.

The film moguls reasoned that if an album by Group A sold a million copies in America alone, then all the fans of Group A would necessarily flock to witness their work in a major motion picture. The film moguls were wrong. Witness The Village People in the dreadful disco movie *Can't Stop The Music*, The Bee Gees and Peter Frampton, amongst others who ought to have known better, in Robert Stigwood's appalling production of *Sgt Pepper's Lonely Hearts Club Band* and the Olivia Newton-John/ELO turkey *Xanadu*.

Occasionally it did work. Ry Cooder found a flourishing new career with his soundtracks for *The Long Riders, Paris, Texas* and *The Border*; while Randy Newman's scores for *Ragtime* and *The Natural* received Oscar nominations and Robert Altman's imaginative use of Leonard

Cohen's songs in *McCabe And Mrs Miller* greatly enhanced the film's atmosphere.

Waits had his own office on the Zoetrope lot, and it was while working at the studio that he met his future wife, script editor Kathleen Brennan. According to Waits' colourful recollections, it wasn't an orthodox courtship: "She can lie down on nails, stick a knitting needle through her lip and still drink coffee, so I knew she was the girl for me." Kathleen Brennan was born and raised in Johnsburg, Illinois, which helped explain one of the most touching fragments of 'Swordfishtrombones'.

The couple were married in August 1980 and honeymooned in Tralee, Co. Kerry. The wedding ceremony itself was not without incident, as Waits remembered when I asked him: "I found the Marriage Chapel in the Yellow Pages, right next to 'Massage'. The registrar's name was Watermelon and he kept calling me Mr Watts! My mother likes what I do, I guess she's happier now that I'm married. I think she was a little bit worried about me for a while."

Waits admitted to me that he was an incredibly undisciplined writer before he began work at Zoetrope, but the experience of scoring a full length feature together with Coppola's generous hands-on involvement helped Waits discipline himself and his songwriting. He told David McGee of *The Record*: "Film scoring is like writing songs for someone else's dream. Up till then, writing songs was something I did when I'd been drinking, and I wasn't absolutely sure I was capable of doing it in terms of being a craftsman. And being part of something very large, you have to discuss openly what it is you do and how it relates to a carpenter, a lighting guy and an actor. So it made me more responsible and more disciplined."

One From The Heart just grew and grew; the finished budget was somewhere around $26 million which has yet to be recouped. The film was by no means a failure, although some critics seemed to resent that the full panoply of Zoetrope hardware should be focused on such a slight story. But the film's charm lies in its very simplicity, the weaving fable of the star-crossed lovers drifting around the garish lights of Las Vegas, all of which was spectacularly brought to life on the Zoetrope lot. The finished film is an audacious fantasy, appropriately filmed on the same sound stages which 40 years before had played host to Michael Powell's lurid and imaginative *The Thief Of Baghdad*, Coppola's favourite film.

From the very first moment when the blue curtains part on screen to their coming together at the end, the film's theatricality is one of its strengths. *One From The Heart* is self-indulgence transformed into high art; while technically spellbinding, with Coppola's use of cross-cuts, montage, fades, parallel narrative and models, at the very heart of the film is the romance between Hank and Franny, which the technology is never allowed to overshadow. It is the very ordinariness of the characters which helps make the film so quietly moving, for while Frederic Forrest may dally with the elusive, enchanted figure of Nastassia Kinski, and Teri Garr seek sanctuary with the tangoing Raul Julia, they eventually find their only real happiness with each other.

69

The extraordinary ordinariness of the relationship which made up *One From The Heart* was puzzling to many of its detractors. Used to films which prided themselves on labyrinthine plots and complex relationships, they sensed an emptiness here, failing to see that the deliberate simplicity of Coppola's love story was in fact its strongest point. What makes *One From The Heart* so visually compelling is Coppola's determination to play out the fantasy against his own lurid recreation of Las Vegas.

Waits had himself been fascinated by Las Vegas for some years, a fascination fuelled by his work on the abortive project with Guy Peellaert. He spoke of his fascination for the city to Richard Rayner of *Time Out* in 1985: "That is the only place where I've ever seen false teeth in a pawn shop window. And prosthetic devices. I've seen a guy sell his glass eye for just one more roll. It's in the middle of nowhere, a graveyard for performers, like a parody of the American Dream. All very confusing, you can be a shoe-shine boy in the morning, a millionaire by noon. More often it works the other way. It's insane."

The songs Waits wrote for the movie are some of his most haunting. Crystal Gayle seemed at first an unlikely choice to sing them, but her pristine voice is an ideal vehicle for Waits' material, and incongruously her clear high vocals blend sublimely with Waits' gravel-voiced delivery.

The odd couple on record play off each other as more than chalk and cheese. Waits' growly timbre speaks for his characters who 'are all in the gutter, but some of us are looking at the stars.' When Crystal Gayle sings a Tom Waits song in *One From The Heart*, she sings from the stars back to the gutter. In her pure unembellished voice come across the dreams and aspirations, the wishes and desires of Hank and Franny. On paper, the pairing of Tom Waits and Crystal Gayle must have seemed like a blind date gone horribly wrong; on record they make it sound so true.

Fired by Coppola's enthusiasm, Waits' songs really do help in furthering the narrative and enabling the characters to develop, and even on record, heard without benefit of the images, the melodies he supplied to fuel Coppola's vision are among his most beguiling.

'Old Boyfriends', 'Take Me Home' and 'Broken Bicycles' are some of Waits' loveliest tunes, while 'Little Boy Blue' and 'You Can't Unring A Bell' feature some of his cleverest lyrics. The poignancy of the line in 'Broken Bicycles': 'Somebody must have an orphanage for all these things that nobody wants any more' and the images in 'Old Boyfriends' – 'like burned out lights on a Ferris wheel' – are vivid and specific. The discipline of working on a film and the challenge of writing songs for someone else to sing gave Waits' work a fiery finish.

It was a time consuming process though, like the old time producer who looked into the aptly named Writers Block on a studio lot: "Call themselves writers? I looked at them for an hour and they didn't write a word!" But once locked into the system Waits' muse didn't desert him. His singing too was ideally suited, the grave sinister reading of 'You Can't Unring A Bell' and the smoky jazzy rendering of 'This One's From The Heart' all added another level to Coppola's film.

While the finished film was flawed, there was no denying that Waits contribution was substantial and it certainly enhanced his standing in the film community. Waits dutifully donned a tuxedo and attended the 1982 Oscars ceremony where his *One From The Heart* music had been nominated as 'Best Original Song Score', only to see it lose to Leslie Bricusse and Henry Mancini's forgettable music for *Victor/Victoria*.

Among the innumerable, unrealised Zoetrope projects Coppola had planned, and one which Waits would have given his best pair of winkle-pickers to be involved in, was a film version of Kerouac's *On The Road* to have been directed by Jean-Luc Godard. But like so many of the dreams that flew over the Zoetrope lot, it was sadly never to make it to the screen.

Waits seemed to enjoy doing film work. His song 'Invitation To The Blues' was used by director Nic Roeg over the end credits of his film *Bad Timing* and Ralph Waite's film *On The Nickel* had a theme song from Waits. He donned his acting hat in 1981 for a blink and you miss him role in *Wolfen*, a rather cumbersome ecological nightmare thriller which starred Albert Finney and was directed by Michael Wadleigh, his first film since the documentary *Woodstock* a decade before; the finished film also used Waits' song 'Jitterbug Boy' on its soundtrack. Waits broke surface again in the rarely seen 1982 Robert Duvall film *The Stone Boy*, which co-starred Glenn Close in an early role; Duvall and Close were the parents of a son who killed his brother, "holding back their emotions in the over-emotional fashion that is the norm for this sort of tear-jerker" wrote one critic. Waits was simply identified as 'petrified man in carnival'.

With time off for good behaviour from Zoetrope, Waits was able to spend two months in Hollywood in mid-1980 recording what turned out to be his final Asylum album. According to Waits, the album was "Me trying to avoid using a knife and fork and a spoon. It wasn't 100 per cent successful, but it's usually the small breakthroughs that give you a tunnel to laterally make some kind of transition. The title track was a breakthrough for me, using that kind of Yardbirds fuzz guitar, having the drummer using sticks instead of brushes, small things like that. More or less putting on a different costume."

'Heartattack And Vine' (which had been provisionally titled 'White Spades') again had Waits relying more on guitar than piano, with his voice sounding more wasted than ever. In its review *New Musical Express* wrote "Waits' voice no longer sounds like it's simply been lived in – more like it's been squatted in by 13 separate Puerto Rican junkie families with tubercular in-laws ... This man's so great he can even give a hangover a sense of dignity!" As ever, Waits was dredging up songs that other writers would avoid like a dead dog.

The title track is a jagged after-hours look at Los Angeles, similar in some ways to 'A Sweet Little Bullet From A Pretty Blue Gun' from 'Blue Valentine', on which Waits railed against Hollywood swindling people out of their dreams. All those wide-eyed innocents who flocked from Iowa and Nebraska to the sacred Hollywood sign, waiting to be discovered at Schwabe's drug store, only to end up in sad, deflowered disillusionment.

The whole album is a distorted glimpse at the City of Angels: vignettes gaudily illuminated by the flashing neon signs of cheap hotels on the Strip and played out against the soundtrack of a screaming police siren. The craziness Waits sings of on 'Til The Money Runs Out' – 'With a pint of green chartreuse, ain't nothin' seems right, you buy the Sunday paper on a Saturday night' – is everywhere, but 'Heartattack And Vine' also includes three of Waits' most beautiful songs: 'Ruby's Arms', a heartbreaking adieu to a love who lies sleeping as he disappears with her scarf as a souvenir, 'On The Nickel' and 'Jersey Girl'.

Bruce Springsteen made a point of including Waits' 'Jersey Girl' in his concerts soon after the Waits version first appeared on vinyl and having re-written the last verse, he recorded it in 1984 and released a live version from a concert at Meadowlands, his home base in New Jersey. The song was a natural choice for New Jersey's most fortunate son and many of the fans assume it is one of his own, just listen to them baying when Bruce sings the line: 'Cause tonight I'm gonna take that ride, across the river to

72

the Jersey side.' Waits joined Springsteen and the E. Street Band on-stage to perform the song at the LA Sports Arena in August 1981, David and Goliath joined at last.

Waits had actually written the song for his wife Kathleen, who before her marriage had settled in New Jersey and the composer's own version on 'Heartattack And Vine' was a most affecting one. Direct and sincere, it avoided Waits' lyrical ambiguities of the time, clearly this too was one from the heart. Melodically, the opening seemed to owe a debt to The Doors' 'The End', but from the moment Waits weighed in with 'Got no time for the corner boys ...', he alone was holding the reins.

In 1986, Springsteen assured Waits of further comfortable royalties when he included the song as the final track on his marathon five-album live package. When I met Waits, he noticed that his modest London shows were to clash with the Boss' residency at Wembley Arena. "He's a nice guy, sure hope that my shows don't detract from his ticket sales," he quipped.

To Bill Flanagan in 1987, Waits responded: "Bruce Springsteen? Well, I've done all I can for him. He's on his own now ... God, I love his songs, I wish I had written 'Meeting Across The River'. His early songs are like little black and white films. Things like 'Wild Billy's Circus Story' were real well-crafted. He's got a great visual sense, a great balance."

Probably the most haunting song on 'Heartattack And Vine' was 'On The Nickel', the title song for Ralph Waite's 1979 film. Waite, best known as the crusty patrician of TV's *The Waltons* starred in, wrote, produced and directed the film about bums on LA's Skid Row. When you're down and out, and there's nowhere lower you can sink, you go 'on the nickel'. Waits' song is a touching nursery rhyme for the derelicts, a hobo's lullaby, reminding us that however far down you slip, you must have begun somewhere as some mother's son. That's what 'becomes of all the little boys who never comb their hair, they're lined up all around the block, on the nickel over there.' The version of the song used in the film has the lines 'You never know how rich you are, you haven't got a prayer/ Heads you win, tails they lose, on the nickel over there' which never made it onto the album.

'Heartattack And Vine' had a harder, R&B edge to it, which balanced the lush orchestrations of 'On The Nickel' and 'Jersey Girl' but it was to be Waits' final album for Asylum. Asked by *New Musical Express*'s Kristine McKenna why he quit Asylum, Waits replied: "Record companies are like large department stores. I was at Elektra for over 10 years and while I was there I spent a considerable amount of time on the road and blowing my own horn. They liked dropping my name in terms of me being a 'prestige' artist, but when it came down to it, they didn't invest a whole lot in me in terms of faith. Their identity was always more aligned with that California rock thing."

In 1981, after he'd quit the label, Asylum released 'Bounced Checks' which included alternative masters of both 'Jersey Girl' and 'Whistlin' Past The Graveyard' as well as a live 'Piano Has Been Drinking' from Dublin and the otherwise unavailable, bluesy 'Mr Henry'. It was a workmanlike compilation, but didn't really do justice to the scope of Waits' seven Asylum albums.

Waits' disenchantment with the music business had been fuelled by his experiences at Zoetrope, and he had found himself dogged by management problems which now culminated in an acrimonious split from long-time manager Herb Cohen, who nevertheless retained the publishing rights to many of his best songs. Perhaps it was just as well that post production work on *One From The Heart* ate up the time.

Waits undertook another European tour in 1981, which included an epic all-night drinking session with Brian Case and Tom Sheehan of *Melody Maker* and the Lesbian Eskimo Chapter of Hell's Angels in an after hours bar in Copenhagen. I remember seeing his concert in London that March at the Apollo, Victoria, the tiny figure appeared to be welded to the piano. His between songs raps made you feel like you were eavesdropping on someone who spoke in their sleep – what was that about someone who fractured a rib in Italy, an ambulance siren and the bridge to 'Over The Rainbow' again?

It seemed appropriate that while Waits was on-stage at the Apollo, the Hayward Gallery was mounting an Edward Hopper retrospective; the two great communicators of American loneliness in London at the same time.

Waits still provided great copy, and journalists queued to get the hip from the lip:

WAITSISMS:

"I'd rather have a bottle in front of me than a frontal lobotomy."

"I don't have a drink problem, 'cept when I can't get a drink."

"I'm so broke I can't even pay attention."

"Champagne for my real friends, real pain for my sham friends."

"I've been busier than a one-armed bass player."

"I don't care who I have to step on on my way down."

"I'm getting harder than Chinese algebra."

"There ain't no devil, there's just God when he's drunk."

"I'm a jack-off of all trades."

"I'm not a household word, I'm just a legend in my own mind."

"You have to keep busy. After all, no dog's ever pissed on a moving car."

"Everybody I like is either dead or not feeling very well."

Waits' career was rolling into the eighties. The singer-songwriter could now add actor, raconteur, *bon viveur*, wit and family man to his CV. The end of the seventies had seen Waits quit smoking, move to New York and turn 30, a transition which left him typically unphased: "The big ages are

16, 33 and a third, 45 and 78!" Waits' 1981 trip to 'Heartattack And Vine' was just a detour, there was a road map up his sleeve that would yet dumbfound the fans and dazzle even his sharpest critics.

CHAPTER FIVE

Tom Waits' Favourite Piece Of Graffiti:

Seen written on the toilet wall of the 'Dark Side Of The Moon' Club in, predictably, East St Louis: "Love is blind; God is love; therefore Ray Charles must be God!"

On his way 'Straight To The Top' Waits must have also seen the following written on a toilet wall somewhere: "To do is to be – Rousseau; To be is to do – Sartre; Doobedoobedoobedoo – Sinatra."

77

Our hero enters his 34th year. For nearly a decade he has accrued a reputation as the bard of the downtrodden. Wherever there was a derelict, went the legend, Tom Waits was there writing a song about him. Fact is, when he's not flexing those tubercular lungs, the man can write some fine songs, they said. Great melodies, but when he starts to sing ...

Got a way with words though, sonofabitch's funny, that one about "the only drink problem I got's when I can't get a drink" always goes down well at closing time. Fact is, that at approximately 1983, most men would be far happier going for a drink with Tom Waits than with Boy George; hell, least you know which toilet Waits is gonna piss in. Thing is, if it's good enough for the Boss, good enough for me, they say.

The way Waits sees it, he's on a one-way ticket to Palookaville. Kerouac slid off the bar stool, Waits slid in. He can regale crowds with his lowlife observations, his saxophonist can play like a siren and split the night in half. Waits can bring the house down, but now he's scrubbing down round the foundations looking to build. From the bottom, things are looking up.

He has at least resisted the temptation which he confided to me of releasing an album called 'My Favorites'. "Like cover versions of your favourite songs, Tom?" "Nah, I'm gonna take 12 songs by other artists and put them on a record, stuff like 'Lady Of Spain', 'Tutti Frutti', The Rolling Stones' 'Just Wanna See His Face' and 'Rudy My Dear' and a picture of me on the cover listening to them!"

He is a calmed down, slowed-down version of the derelict who carved a niche at the Tropicana. Jack Kerouac remains an idol, but not a role model. Tom is now called 'daddy' by his first child Kelly Simone, born in 1983. He has relocated to New York, he has cut three tracks – 'Shore Leave', 'Frank's Wild Years' and '16 Shells From A Thirty-Ought-Six' – which are quite unlike anything he has ever attempted before. These are staccato windbreaks, daemonic howlings floating over the walls of the asylum. They're the tunes the Pied Piper plays, and the rats follow his floating tune, but Asylum executives stare at each other blank-faced and ask: who wants an audience of rats?

The songs are sufficiently left-field to let Waits' out of his Asylum contract and move to Island. Label boss Chris Blackwell needs just one listen to know that Waits and Island are going to get along just fine. Waits' collector John Green somehow managed to obtain an Australian Asylum pressing of 'Swordfishtrombones' – only 50 copies of which were ever pressed – with a cover drawing by Waits in the style of Picasso, that's Kevin Picasso of course, not Pablo.

Before the mad dog that is called 'Swordfishtrombones' can be let off its chain though, Tom Waits has some other business to finish. So he shakes the dust off his Henry Irving cloak and makes with the soliloquies.

Mentor Francis Ford Coppola had forged ahead with Zoetrope Studios after the disappointing box office receipts for *One From The Heart* and Waits had remained fascinated by the possibilities posed by the movies. During 1983, Coppola was fired by the works of teenage novelist Susan (S.E.) Hinton, and rushed through his own films of two of her novels – *The Outsiders* and *Rumble Fish*, both of which feature appearances from Tom Waits.

Waits has long been a movie fan; he remembers as a kid in LA going regularly to one cinema which he claimed showed the most unlikely double bills – would you believe *101 Dalmatians* playing with *The Pawnbroker?* Years later, when asked, Waits went on to name a motley collection of his favourite films including Fellini's *La Strada* and *8 1/2*, Kurosawa's *Ikuru*, Disney's *Snow White* and Stanley Baker's *Zulu!* When pressed, he will muster Peter O'Toole and Jack Nicholson among his favourite actors, and among directors, Alfred Hitchcock, Martin Scorsese, Jim Jarmusch and, of course, Francis Ford Coppola.

Coppola called *Rumble Fish* "An art film for kids. It doesn't have to be *Porky's* ... *The Outsiders* and *Rumble Fish* are heroic epics for 14-year-olds." Waits told Brian Case: "In *Rumble Fish* I play Bennie of Bennie's Pool Hall, I'm like Doc at the Maltshop ... you know? It's where the kids hang out, it's my joint, keep ya feet off the tables, knock it off, watch ya language. I got a chance to pick my own costume and write my own dialogue. Gotta nice scene with a clock ... Time is a funny thing. Sometimes you wish you could take the time when you have the time, put it somewhere, save it, because there's times when you haven't got time. Spend it there. Ahhh – you kids! Gotta full life ahead of ya. I've had 35 summers. That's all. Think about it."

On being asked how he coped with the transition from musician to actor, Waits replied: "It's like going from bootlegging to watch repair. *Rumble Fish* was like a fractured teenage opium dream. In *The Outsiders* I

79

had one line: 'What is it you boys want?' I still have it down if they need me to go back and recreate the scene for any reason.''

Coppola's two black and white films of 1983 tried to address America's youth constituency without patronising them, but sadly neither *The Outsiders* nor *Rumble Fish* reached an audience which seemed more interested in *I Gouge Out Your Eyes* or *Nymphomaniac Teenage Bimbettes*.

Outside of *The Magnificent Seven*, 1983's *The Outsiders* featured the most star-studded cast of unknowns in Hollywood: Emilio Estevez (*Young Guns*), Patrick Swayze (*Dirty Dancing*), Tom Cruise (*Top Gun*), Matt Dillon (*The Flamingo Kid*), Ralph Macchio (*The Karate Kid*). But for all the cast's youthful vigour and the film's valiant efforts to recreate James Dean type rebels in a sixties setting through eighties eyes, and even in spite of Tom Waits' line, Coppola's film still fell flat.

Rumble Fish was far more successful, largely thanks to Mickey Rourke's ethereal Motorcycle Boy, whose phantom presence haunts the film. Coppola called the film "Camus for kids," and while pumped full of outsider stereotypes, Rumble Fish managed to convey a finite sense of time, place and motivation. Waits' character displayed a grisly line in shirts, specs and hats. As Benny he constantly grumbled at all the kids hanging round "mind your language." While not exactly a character acting scene-stealer like Walter Brennan, Waits was moving further up the credits and was getting bigger roles than 'saloon bum'. He still complained though that the only roles he was being offered were "drunk Irish piano players ... and Satanist cult leaders."

Festering in Waits' fertile imagination were plans for something that would distance him from his past as Bowery bum and place his winkle-pickered foot on the ladder of the future. Inevitably though, when he was asked to explain the title of his watershed ninth album, the composer could only explain thus: "'Swordfishtrombones' is either a musical instrument that smells bad, or a fish that makes a lot of noise!"

Waits' album sounded like a rag and bone man sifting through the detritus of a junkyard, hubcaps banged and pipe organs wheezed on instrumentals sounding like snatches snitched from Dante's Inferno. With rock music elsewhere becoming cosily androgynous, increasingly relying on the impact of the promo video and emphatically placing style over content, Tom Waits was moving alone into territory that hadn't yet been mapped.

I remember the shock of the new when I first heard 'Swordfishtrombones'. For me, the Waits that registered was the keyboard balladeer; ol' gravel-voice, musing aloud as he sat 'wasted and wounded' in an anonymous hotel bar. The Waits' songs that relied on his piano accompaniment swelled by a lush orchestra were, for me, the pinnacle. Songs such as 'Jersey Girl' and 'On The Nickel', 'Ol' 55' and 'The Heart Of Saturday Night'; sentimental journeys perhaps, but perfectly balanced by Waits' definitely unsentimental readings. Listening to the percussive stabbing of 'Swordfishtrombones' was like being knocked unconscious by a pile of 78s you'd forgotten you had.

That it was innovative I could appreciate; that it was at odds with anything else around went without saying; but it also sounded inescapably as if Waits was deliberately and perversely alienating his audience. And while I could not but admire the boldness of his stand, that didn't necessarily mean I was going to enjoy it.

At times, during the period bordered by 'Swordfishtrombones' and 'Frank's Wild Years', it sounded like Waits was becoming a growling parody of himself. That he was no longer living the life of the motel minstrel which had fuelled his early albums was obvious, listening to his three alienating Island albums it sounded like Waits had got himself cast instead as the Creature From Another Planet, occasionally falling from the sky over Earth to see how it was getting on in his absence.

But like all the best scenarios, this one too had a happy ending. Even amidst the hammering there were fine examples of the Waits I loved: 'In The Neighbourhood', 'Soldier's Things', 'Hang Down Your Head', 'Time', 'Cold Cold Ground' and 'Train Song' were fine examples of Waits at his most convincing. If the other pieces on these albums didn't strike such a responsive chord in me, there was still plenty to admire in them, and out of admiration, a curious sort of affection soon began to develop.

'Swordfishtrombones' was like a changeling you found on your doorstep, only in adulthood did it reveal its true colours, and by then you loved it for what it was, not what it claimed to be. By the time of the release of 'Swordfishtrombones' in 1983, Tom Waits was guaranteed space on my turntable whatever deviationist tactics he was employing.

Pogue Jem Finer has an interesting theory about the title of 'Swordfishtrombones': he remembers reading to his children from an American illustrated alphabet book, 'Woodpecker' and 'Xylophone' were the examples spread over two adjoining pages and he's convinced that Tom Waits had a similar book for his daughter, with 'Swordfish' and 'Trombone' as the selected examples for 'S' and 'T'!

Elvis Costello told me in 1989: "When the records 'Swordfishtrombones' and 'Rain Dogs' came out, I thought it was a very brave move, because he had such a totally complete persona, based around this hipster thing he'd taken from Kerouac and Bukowski, and the music was tied to some Beat/Jazz thing, and suddenly it's exploring music that was something to do with Howlin' Wolf and Charles Ives. I think I was envious, not so much of the music, but his ability to rewrite himself out of the corner he'd appeared to have backed himself into. It was an audacious thing to do, and I think that anyone who can't recognise the quality of that music really doesn't have their ears on the right way round!" Costello was not alone in being bowled over by Waits' assured change of pace.

Waits acknowledged that expatriate British jazz-man Victor Feldman had a lot to do with the album's unique sound. "He suggested instruments I wouldn't have considered – squeeze drums, Balinese percussion, calliopes, glass harmonica, marimba – things I've always been timid about. Anthony Clark-Stewart played the bagpipes, looked like he was strangling a goose!"

Waits also thought it significant that it was the first of his albums not to feature saxophone; with this album he truly was leaving 'jazz' behind and going off on his own, trawling through the flotsam and jetsam of American music. Waits had become fascinated by the sounds and textures which make up music, he wanted the sound of Captain Beefheart colliding head-on in a wind-tunnel with Charles Ives, while Slim Dusty and Howlin'

Wolf stood by and watched. Waits explained the genesis of
'Swordfishtrombones' as listening "to the noise in my head and inventing
some junkyard orchestral deviation ... it's a demented journal ... an
odyssey of exotic design."

Hovering phantom-like over the whole album is the spirit of composer
and hobo Harry Partch, the man who invented the monophonic music
scale and designed such instruments as the Mazda Marimba, which
incorporated specially tuned light bulbs. Waits had become fascinated by
Partch's radical attitudes to dissolving and rebuilding music: "Francis
Thumm is an old companion of mine, he is a professor and he plays the
crumelodian in The Harry Partch Ensemble ... Partch was an American
hobo and the instruments he made were all built from things that he
essentially found on the side of the road, not literally but figuratively. He
dismantled and rebuilt his own version of the whole concept of music and
its purpose, but I just like the sounds he makes."

Harry Partch was already 34 when he hit the road in 1935, he would
spend the next eight years on the bum, living the kind of life Waits would
later recreate in *Ironweed*. Partch had begun composing when he was only
14, but in his late twenties grew disillusioned with all his work, and
destroyed the lot.

A musical Luddite, he became fascinated by the possibilities of starting
from scratch and, on his travels around the States during the Depression,
began building his own instruments, none of which ever needed electricity.
In his mid-forties, Partch began recording using only his own hand-built
instruments, like the kithera, a lyre with 72 strings and enormous bamboo
reeds called boos. 'The World Of Harry Partch' album included the typical
'Eight Hitch-Hiker Inscriptions From A Highway Railing At Barstow,
California'. Partch died in 1974 in San Diego, and remained a largely
neglected figure until Waits began to champion his work during the
eighties.

To *Playboy*, Waits waxed lyrical about Partch and his influence on his
own music: "Partch was an innovator. He built all his own instruments and
kind of took the American hobo experience and designed instruments
from ideas he gathered travelling around the United States in the thirties

83

and forties. He used a pump organ and industrial water bottles, created enormous marimbas. He died in the early seventies, but the Harry Partch Ensemble still performs at festivals.

"It's a little arrogant to say I see a relationship between his stuff and mine. I'm very crude, but I use things we hear around us all the time, built and found instruments – things that aren't normally considered instruments: dragging a chair across the floor or hitting the side of a locker real hard with a two-by-four, a freedom bell, a brake drum with major imperfection, a police bullhorn. It's more interesting. You know, I don't like straight lines. The problem is that most instruments are square and music is always round."

Whatever its influences, the finished album was undeniably Tom Waits. The hallmarks were unmistakable, whether it was the black humour of 'Frank's Wild Years', the brass band camaraderie of 'In The Neighbourhood' or the sombre reflections of 'Soldier's Things' and 'Johnsburg, Illinois'. Waits likened one song on the album, 'Underground' to "a mutant dwarf community in a steam tunnel," which gives an indication of the composer's fertile imagination.

Waits' cut-up technique, the fractured song structure and lyrics which spoke of nightmares and drowned dreams, all enhanced an album that sounded like it was recorded in a forge. Nothing Waits had done before prepared you for this. 'Swordfishtrombones' didn't make for comfortable listening, but then nothing with bagpipes in it ever does.

The acute eye for detail was wide open again, most notably on the tragedy of 'Soldier's Things' in which Waits sifts through the detritus of one veteran's life in a crummy garage sale: 'Oh, and this one is for bravery/ and this one is for me/ and everything's a dollar in this box.' On 'Town With No Cheer', Waits went walkabout in the great Australian outback. Borrowing his song structure from that wonderful alternative Australian national anthem, 'A Pub With No Beer', Waits surprised Australian band The Triffids with his authentic evocation of the outback.

'In The Neighbourhood' was lifted as Waits' first Island single, which came complete with atmospheric video directed by cinematographer Haskell Wexler, whose credits included *American Graffiti* and *One Flew*

Over The Cuckoo's Nest. Shot through a fisheye lens in beautiful sepia tones, Waits was shown as a top-hatted carney leading a ragged band of misfits through the neighbourhood in question; if they weren't all friends of Waits, they looked exactly like the sort of crowd who would turn up at his house to make a fourth hand at bridge.

'Swordfishtrombones' was the first album Waits had produced himself. Prodded on the matter he admitted, "I get dressed by myself in the morning, so I figured I could look after the music on my own as well." Paul Young took 'Soldier's Things' and included it on his smash 1984 LP 'The Secret Of Association', although the songwriter was credited as one 'T. Waite'.

'Swordfishtrombones' is Waits' own Zoetrope: his camera weaves and roves, probes and pulls back from the neighbourhood, there's Dave the Butcher, here's Kurt Weill being shown the way to the next whisky bar. Charles Ives and Harry Partch are busking on berserk instruments, a soldier's holding a pathetic sale of his past, the sailors are on shore leave in mayhem. In the arid Australian outback the pub with no beer makes a town without cheer. There's heartbreak in a small town in Illinois. It's raining and the Sedan's wipers are plainly unable to cope, the only light comes from a blazing home illuminating a character Waits would soon get to know a lot better.

Frank Leroux is first introduced hanging his 'wild years on a nail that he drove through his wife's forehead' before torching everything, hitting the Hollywood Freeway and heading north. 'Frank's Wild Years' is a minute-and-a-half snatch of something far bigger. Waits claimed that the original inspiration for the song came from a Charles Bukowski short story about how it's usually the little things that push people to the very brink: in Frank's case, a blind Chihuahua called Carlos with a skin disease! Frank was to grow up on 'Rain Dogs' two years later and would get his very own show and album in 1987; but for the time being, the last we see of Frank is driving that old Sedan, barrelling down the boulevard, backlit by the blazing timbers of what had been his home; and the dog it was that died.

Around the time of the release of 'Swordfishtrombones', Waits revealed that his own favourite compositions included two songs from this most recent album, the instrumental 'Dave The Butcher' and 'In The Neighbourhood'. He also expressed a strong paternal affection for 'Tom Traubert's Blues' and 'Burma Shave'. Of the album as a whole, Waits reflected: "Things like 'Frank's Wild Years' worked but sometimes a story can be too dry and alone. I'm getting to where I want to see things where either the words are more concise so that the picture I am trying to create becomes more clear, or be more vague in description and allow the music to take the listener to the place where you want them to go. I've been working in film recently and there are so many departments, this enormous committee making decisions about illusion."

It was Francis Ford Coppola who reconvened the committee when he organised Waits' membership of *The Cotton Club*. As on every project he became involved with, Coppola's very appearance on set seemed to send the budgets rocketing. Initially drafted in just to re-write Mario Puzo's script, Coppola eventually wound up in charge of the whole $47 million project, which went through 38 separate screenplay drafts before its completion.

The movie fell into the quagmire that the film industry seemed so prone to during the eighties. The decade had begun badly with the precedent of Michael Cimino's spiralling *Heaven's Gate*, and had tumbled on through films like *Revolution, Howard The Duck, Labyrinth* and *Ishtar*, each with a budget big enough to subsidise a dozen meritorious independent movies. Clinging desperately to this deeply flawed 'Big Is Beautiful' mentality, producers juggled the stars' inflating egos and their escalating budgets, and wound up with lifeless, empty artefacts like *The Cotton Club*.

Fired with enthusiasm from working with eager young casts on the quick, low-budget *Outsiders* and *Rumble Fish*, Coppola immediately ran into problems with producer Robert Evans. Used to being the ringmaster at Zoetrope, Coppola found it hard buckling down to being a hired hand again. Ambitious and unwieldy, *The Cotton Club* lacked focus, the Club itself should have been at the centre of the film, but instead it ended up as a cumbersome cross between *Once Upon A Time In America* and *Guys And Dolls*.

On its release in 1984, *The Cotton Club* was slammed. Jazz fans were far better served by *Round Midnight* and *Bird*, and it was now apparent that the combination of Coppola and Puzo had failed to rekindle the spark which fired *The Godfather* a decade before. The public showed little interest in the place where the publicists boasted "crime lords rub elbows with the rich and famous."

The film failed on virtually every level. Richard Gere was unbelievable as the cornet-playing hero, there were some eye-catching dance routines, but with a budget that could sustain 50 dance companies for a year, so there ought to be. The finished film was an ineffectual mix of tap-dancing and gang warfare; above all it lacked atmosphere, the smoky whiff of danger and drama never got beyond the celluloid club's front door. As Waits' character remarked at one point in the film, "these are the times sent to try men's souls."

The irony of the real Cotton Club was that it was New York's premier showcase for black talent between 1923 and 1936, but only whites were allowed in to watch. The Harlem nightspot was where Duke Ellington and Cab Calloway polished their routines before rich white crowds 'putting on the ritz'.

Waits said he spent 10 weeks in a tuxedo for his bit part in *The Cotton Club* ("it was like being Shanghaied") and his role may well have amounted to more, but with daily re-writes, he was gradually elbowed from the finished film. In all, Waits as cigar-chewing club manager Irving Stark mustered only around a dozen lines, some of which he relished delivering through a bullhorn.

The only two principals to emerge with any semblance of dignity were Fred Gwynne and Bob Hoskins who realised a lifetime's ambition by acting opposite 'Herman Munster'. Waits was already a big fan of Hoskins', he'd relished his performance in the BBC series *Pennies From Heaven* when it was screened on American TV. A final word on the prohibitively expensive flop of *The Cotton Club*: like the man said "Jazz? Delicious hot, disgusting cold!"

While 'Swordfishtrombones' had been met with great critical acclaim on its release in 1983, Tom Waits still wasn't exactly making millions part with the folding. He was asked by Kristine McKenna if it was a goal of his to have a hit single? "I don't know that you should wish for things you don't understand, for reasons that you question. A hit single means that you make a lot of money and a lot of people will know who you are, and I don't know that that's so attractive.

"I don't see the importance of having your face on a lunchbox in Connecticut. I don't see how that fits into the grand scheme of things as something to strive for ... A lot of people are looking for affection and acceptance in the form of this anonymous group of people thinking they're wonderful. People they don't even know. You don't want to choose your friends arbitrarily."

While to David McGee he came up with a suitably Waitsian evocation of his career to date: "A career's like having a dog you can kick. Sometimes it jumps up on you when you're all dressed up and you have to scold it – 'Get down boy'. And other times it runs away and you can't find it and it ends up in the pound and you have to spend all this money to get it out. So that's my dog. My career's my dog."

His current canine wouldn't lie down, it kept coming back to Waits, tail-wagging and eager to be stroked. Gruff and cantankerous, Waits kept kicking it away, couldn't help but admire the damn creature's persistence though.

While Waits kept notebooks full of lines and song titles, much of his actual writing was now done in the studio, and while he beavered away on a worthy follow-up to the much praised 'Swordfishtrombones', one name kept recurring.

Carlos the Chihuahua's funeral pyre had seemed pretty terminal in 1983, but Waits and his wife Kathleen found themselves still fascinated by the character and peculiar obsessions of Frank Leroux. What was it that really drove an ordinary, regular guy like Frank to torch the family home, and where would he go from there?

In May 1985, Waits was still speculating enthusiastically about the song and the character to Barney Hoskyns: "'Frank's Wild Years'... is bent and misshapen and tawdry and warm ... something for all the family ... Frank goes to Las Vegas and becomes a spokesman for an all-night clothing store. He wins a talent contest and some money on the crap tables, but then he gets rolled by a cigarette girl, and – despondent and penniless – he finds an accordion in a trashcan, and one thing leads to another, and before you know it he's on-stage. Y'see, when he was a kid, Frank's parents ran a funeral parlour, and while his mother did hair and makeup for the passengers, Frank played accordion. So he'd already started a career in showbiz as a child."

While the Waits' were being drawn further into the quirky world of Frank Leroux, and with no unreleased Waits material in their vaults, his old label had taken the opportunity to recycle 20 of his best known songs on the double 1984 package 'The Asylum Years'; it was a competent compilation, spanning his career from the innocent nostalgia of 'Ol' 55' through to the down and out lullaby of 'On The Nickel'. The album was an adequate pair of bookends on Waits' career to 1980, but it was obviously just an echo of where Tom Waits had been, where he was going hadn't been written about yet.

Waits' old songs also featured in *Streetwise*, Martin Bell's brutal 1984 documentary film about teenage kids 'on the nickel' in Seattle. It was a harrowing account of young kids involved in dope and prostitution, incest and crime, shot in a vivid cinema verity style.

Two years on from the triumph of 'Swordfishtrombones', in 1985, Waits became a father again. Initially tempted to christen his first son 'Senator' ("Senator Waits sounds good") or 'Ajax', he and Kathleen eventually settled on Casey Xavier. As a parent, Waits relished the role of stern disciplinarian, insisting that his family line up and salute him every morning before he packed them off to military school. Least that's what the old tiger said ...

Waits' new album finally hit the racks, it was entitled 'Rain Dogs' and picked up neatly where 'Swordfishtrombones' left off. After deciding against 'Evening Train Wrecks', Waits explained the canine title thus: "It's a phenomenon you'll find mostly in Lower Manhattan. After a rainstorm, the dogs get caught. Somehow the water washes away their whole trail and they can't get back home. So about four in the morning you see all these stranded dogs on the street and they look at you like 'Won't you help me, sir, please?'"

The album was more accessible than its predecessor, but contained all the hallmarks which identified Waits' work during the eighties: fractured instrumentation, lyrical obliqueness, a wide term of musical reference and the composer's ability to identify and evaluate quirky characters in his songs, all chronicled in that inimitable voice. "How do you feel about yourself as a vocalist?" "At best I'm a barking dog, but I think my voice is well suited to my material." "Have you taken steps to protect your voice?" "Protect it from what? Vandals?"

Much was made of Keith Richards' contribution to the album, and Waits was typically helpful when asked by Gavin Martin how the Rolling Stone came to contribute: "We're relatives, I didn't realise it. We met in a women's lingerie shop, we were buying brassieres for our wives ... No, he's been borrowing money from me for so long that I had to put a stop to it ... I was going to throw 'Union Square' out, I said call in the dustman, this one's chewing on the dead. But somebody said there's something there. Hell, I said, there isn't. Then he came in – on the clock he stands with his head at three and his arm at 10. I said how can a man stand like that without falling over unless he has a 200lb test fishing line suspending him from the ceiling? It was like something out of *Arthur*!"

Fans of the 'old' Tom Waits were appeased by the beautiful 'Hang Down Your Head', 'Downtown Train' and 'Time', the latter one of his most frail and resounding melodies; while songs such as 'Singapore', 'Tango Till They're Sore' and 'Walking Spanish' followed the exciting new signposts first erected for 'Swordfishtrombones'.

For his new album, Waits dealt lyrics from a pack on which the seal hadn't been broken. 'Time' is a painful fragment of despair and isolation when you're 'East of East St. Louis/ And the wind is making speeches/ And the rain sounds like a round of applause.' Waits' delivery of these sparse lines makes it sound like the most godforsaken spot on the planet. 'Downtown Train' had 'all those Brooklyn girls ... scattering like crows ... thorns without the rose.' While 'Cemetery Polka' had Waits whistling past the graveyard observing, 'Uncle Bill will never leave a will, and the tumour is as big as an egg/ He has a mistress, she's Puerto Rican, and I hear she has a wooden leg.'

The songs prowled the soaking, night-time city streets where the rain dogs parade. They hung around the docks waiting for freighters shipping out to Singapore and caused trouble on the corner of 9th and Hennepin. With 'Rain Dogs', Tom Waits confirmed himself as one of the few genuine musical innovators of the eighties. Resting on your laurels got you a lotta pricks, so it was heigh-ho and off towards the unknown. Here was music that sounded like it came from the decadent cabarets of Weimar Germany, sleazy satire that floated out from Kurfurstendamm clubs before the terrifying crunch of jackboots drowned the music of Brecht and Eisler.

Here was blues that sounded like it had lain in a damp bargain basement, here was jazz the like of which had not seen daylight since Armistice Day, New Orleans marching funeral bands trailing after a hearse with no name. 'Blind Love' was arthritic Country and Western. Mix in Batista era Cuban tangos, tarantellas Columbus could tap his toe to, fractured rhythms from rock 'n' roll, Broadway balladry and sprinkle in a little fresh tarragon before bringing to the boil.

Waits had become fascinated by the sound and texture of music. If Tom Waits wanted the sound of a nail being driven into a lump of wood, he'd wield the hammer himself and mike it up, no sampling for this lumberjack. "Texture is real important to me; it's like attaining grain or putting it a little out of focus. I don't like cleanliness. I like surface noise. It kind of becomes the glue of what you're doing sometimes."

The glue that bonded 'Rain Dogs' together was unique. There was a terrible beauty in Waits' elliptical view of his world and with his determination to precisely capture the individual sound suited to each track, Waits ensured that 'Rain Dogs' scampered in a field all its own.

The album was the first Waits had made entirely in New York, while the family were living between the New York State Armoury and the Salvation Army HQ. As ever, Waits' eclecticism is impressive: the line in 'Singapore' 'In the land of the blind, the one-eyed man is King' came originally from Michael Apostolius' 15th Century Proverbs, and was also

the title of an H. G. Wells short story; 'Clap Hands' picked up where
Shirley Ellis' 'The Clapping Song' left off; the chorus of 'Jockey Full Of
Bourbon' borrowed from nursery rhyme; while the melody of 'Hang
Down Your Head' was already familiar to admirers of the late 'Tom
Dooley'.

'Rain Dogs' has Tom Waits as storyteller *par excellence*. Maybe you
don't quite catch all the words, and the moral's kinda confused, but you
know you're in the teeth of a great yarn. Waits came across as some
crusty, barnacled mariner, he'd stop anyone who'd listen to his tales, a
widely-travelled soak with tales as tall as a mast that you could hear for
the price of a drink.

Determined to foist Waits on a nervous teenage audience, 'Downtown
Train' was lifted from the album and released as a single. Propelled by the
guitar of G. E. Smith (who first emerged as guitarist behind Hall And
Oates in 1980 and accompanied Bob Dylan to great acclaim on his 1988
tour), the stark black and white video opened with the real 'raging bull'
Jake La Motta moaning about Waits singing underneath his window. Waits
gavottes on the rain-drenched streets, hair sticking out like the split in a
horsehair sofa, spindly arms snatching at stars.

What you heard on these songs were but fragments of a far greater
story, which was already mutating into the musical of *Frank's Wild Years*
that would première in Chicago in June 1986.

But Frank himself was already there on 'Rain Dogs', like Henry Fonda
in *The Grapes Of Wrath*: "I'll be all around in the dark. I'll be everywhere
... I'll be in the way guys yell when they're mad – and I'll be in the way kids
laugh when they're hungry and they know supper's ready. And when the
people are eating the stuff they raise, living in the houses they build – I'll
be there too."

'Rain Dogs' was generally hailed as a worthy successor to
'Swordfishtrombones'. U2's Bono even accorded Waits his highest
accolade – "He should have been an Irishman" – when he selected the
album as one of 1985's best; REM's Michael Stipe picked it as his favourite
too, while *Rolling Stone* critics elected Waits their Songwriter of the Year

and The Pogues had the album playing as a cacophonous soundtrack on their tour bus for months.

Waits' 1985 tour saw him playing to packed houses all over Europe. In concert, Waits had to be surgically prised away from the microphone stand: bony limbs akimbo, he barked lyrics into the mike, hat perched at a desperate angle, face like plasticine. Seated at the piano, Waits' extraordinary double-jointed fingers roved the keys, eyes closed, lost in a reverie of sorts, he still sent his voice off on kamikaze missions in search of long unattainable high notes.

Like errant children, Waits' songs on that tour were compelling and infuriating in equal measure. For all the shambling about on-stage, Waits had tight control of his band and was determined that his live work would replicate the studio sound. "At one time," Waits admitted in a moment of customary quirkiness, "I did actually try and put together an entire band of midgets ... I was probably approaching fatherhood."

93

In an era of increasing pomposity and insularity in rock music, Tom Waits' 1985 shows were a particularly welcome example of intimacy and communication. Waits' six nights at the London Dominion that year had critics ransacking their vocabularies for superlatives. Even the trendy *Elle* magazine wrote that "this month's ticket to credibility" was the opportunity to see Waits in concert. Not everyone succumbed to the spell though, *Record Mirror* reader Sean Coyne quibbled that Waits "seemed more like Frank Sinatra's grandfather than the hottest thing to cross the Atlantic in recent months."

And still there was Frank ... "How did 'Frank's Wild Years' turn into a musical?" queried Gavin Martin. "The song was like a fortune cookie, after I wrote it I thought what happened to this guy. Everybody knows guys like that, people you haven't seen in a long time. People go through these permutations in different stages of their life, perceived by someone else it can look strange. I imagined Frank along those lines, y'see my folks split up when I was a kid and ... hey, look, let me give you $100 and I'll lie down on the couch over there, you take notes, and we'll see if we can't get to the bottom of this!"

94

CHAPTER SIX

Nelson Algren characterised the citizens of Chicago as "The nobodies nobody knows, with faces cut from the same cloth as their caps, and the women whose eyes reflect nothing but the pavement." Playwright David Mamet said "Chicago audiences are difficult to fool. They like going to the theatre and having their socks knocked off."

The Windy City was the only place on God's earth to witness *Frank's Wild Years* in all its glory. Chicago was Waits' kinda town, Kathleen had lived there for some years and Waits had been impressed by the work of the city's Steppenwolf Theatre Company.

Tom Waits wasn't giving much away to Frank's Chicago audience. Asked by TV chat show host David Letterman to describe the show, Waits helpfully called it "a cross between Jacqueline Susann's *The Love Machine* and the *New Testament*," and later "a cross between *Eraserhead* and *It's A Wonderful Life*."

The three-month Chicago run of *Frank's Wild Years* in the summer of 1986 played to packed houses and saw Waits on-stage every night in the leading role. The finished play was a full collaboration between Waits and his wife Kathleen, expanding the character of Frank Leroux (renamed Frank O'Brien for the stage play) from the snatched glimpse on 'Swordfishtrombones'.

Frank had become a kind of blank canvas which Tom and Kathleen could fill with all the details and fabrications of a man's life. It was Francis Ford Coppola who had first introduced Waits to the delights of opera and Kathleen came up with the tag 'un operachi romantico' to describe the show. *Frank's Wild Years* wasn't the sort of opera Wagner would recognise though, not for Tom Waits Rhine maidens with their chests puffed out like pigeons. Frank's whole world was bordered by park benches and bars, but Waits believed the show had the feel of "a Biblical story ... one man's redemption and baptism and all that."

Asked by Brian Case in 1987 to try and describe the stage show for those who hadn't been able to make the trip to Chicago, Waits responded: "*Frank's Wild Years* is the story of a guy from a small town who goes out to seek fame and fortune, but he steps on every bucket in the road. Frank's no champion. We start him off on a park bench in East St Louis – despondent, penniless, freezing – but he dreams his way back to the saloon where he began ... All of Frank's shortcomings rise up before him, right in the middle of him bragging in the bar ..."

Waits admitted that he envisaged Frank as a kind of urban Don Quixote, tilting at windmills and wound up in dreams. But while Frank may have been a loser, he was also a survivor and at the end of it all, Frank is at least given another chance. For Waits, Frank is the living denial of Scott Fitzgerald's widely quoted "There are no second acts in American lives."

The play charted Frank's urban odyssey from park bench to bar, the songs acting as a commentary on his state of mind, his aspirations and his illusions. "It's really, simply enough, the story of a guy from a small town who goes out to seek his fame and fortune; a standard odyssey. Eventually, what happens is that he dreams his way back home to the saloon where he began. He's given ... a ticket home, and there he tells the story of his success. But he stops in the middle of it, and tells the real story. He's no hero, he is no champion; wasn't what he says he was. He was, really, a guy who stepped on every bucket on the road. His friends kind of pull him out of it, and tell him he's got plenty to live for. In the end, he wakes up on the bench, ready to start again."

While on his travels, Frank encounters a berserk, blind evangelist (detailed on the song 'Way Down In A Hole') and finds himself in New York as the spokesman for a Vegas haberdashery outfit, Zookie's East, where he is forced to change the lyrics of his song 'Innocent When You Dream' to the more commercial 'In A Suit Of Your Dreams'!

Of the complexities of Frank's travails in the Chicago show, Waits commented: "On-stage, it really is ambiguous, how much you choose to believe, as if the whole re-evaluation of all his shortcomings took place moments before death. It was the snowflake that didn't fall that saved him from hitting the freezing point."

The initial plans to film *Frank's Wild Years* had to be shelved and the costs of mounting a touring production of the play were prohibitive. So in order to salvage some of the ideas from the show, Waits channelled elements of it into the album and tour which were to occupy him for much of 1987.

The album gave a good flavour of the show, and displayed just how diverse Waits' music had become: 'Frank's Wild Years' had everything from Frank Sinatra through Marty Robbins to Irish ballads, from Mexican mariachi to Rudy Vallee. But Waits' strength wasn't just in his musical flamboyance, this wasn't someone showing off with mariachi on one hand and muzak on the other. Waits could familiarise himself with a musical style, nuzzle right inside it, and then burrow his way out with enough shards clinging to him to be able to start from scratch. Waits was the demented ringmaster on Frank, cracking his whip as his charges went through their routines; out of it, but near enough to get right back to the heart of the matter.

When songwriters are asked to talk about their songs, their answers usually fall into one of two categories (1) "I dunno where the songs come from ... it's like ... it's like I'm not writing them, they're not coming from me, they're coming from ... somewhere else" or (2) "I read this book about how you can split the atom with a comb and an elastic band, so I wrote a song about it."

Putting Tom Waits in the witness box and asking him about songwriting was like putting Baron Munchausen under oath and asking him about his holiday plans. Waits' efforts at describing his work were like accompanying him on a tour through a tawdry souvenir shop, each trinket reminding him of something, each snowstorm in a bottle prompting a memory.

For the album of 'Frank's Wild Years', Waits threw away his thoughts on the songs to journalist Rip Rense: 'Hang On St Christopher' ("kind of Jerry Lewis going down on the Titanic ... a depraved Vaudeville train announcer ... kind of mutant James Brown"); 'I'll Be Gone' ("a Tarus Bulba number. Almost like a tarantella ... Part of a pagan ritual we still observe in the Los Angeles area"); 'Yesterday Is Here' ("wanted to get some spaghetti-western feel ... the title was given to me by Fred Gwynne"); 'More Than Rain' ("a little Edith Piaf attempt"); 'I'll Take New York' ("I think it's the closest thing on the record to a nightmare. Guy standing in Times Square with tuberculosis and no money").

Although the proud owner of one of pop's most easily recognisable voices, on this album Waits trades in the hallmark gravel for a more flexible instrument, working hard to tailor it to fit each individual song. He gives 'Hang On St. Christopher' a breathless urgency, while 'Innocent When You Dream' has a naïve, almost child-like quality. 'I'll Take New York' tips its fedora gently in the direction of Francis Albert Sinatra and in concert Waits would preface the song with "I went to the throat doctor, he said 'You can't keep singing like that; you'll end up like Frank Sinatra.' I said 'What, rich and powerful?'" Waits also admitted to having written a song specifically for Hoboken's favourite crooner called 'Empty Pockets', but apparently he had been unable to contact Sinatra: "I guess he's unlisted."

Many of the album's lyrics dealt with the quality of dreams, but there was also plenty of sage Waits advice, such as the following gem on 'Telephone Call From Istanbul': 'Never trust a man in a blue trench coat/ never drive a car when you're dead!'

The pathetic downward spiral of Frank's life is beautifully captured on 'Cold Cold Ground' and 'Train Song', the latter containing the seeds of Frank's decline. Broken down once again, in 'East St Louis', Frank wearily concludes, 'It was a train that took me away from here, but a train can't take me home.' Too much has happened since that first departure, 10,000 miles travelled, with nothing to show for all that distance.

The album concludes with a scratchy version of its most beautiful song, 'Innocent When You Dream', which replicates the sound of a well played 78 rpm record. The song, in waltz time, draws its inspiration from Waits' father-in-law's fondness for Irish singer John McCormack, The Pogues and traditional Irish music. It is played out against soft green fields, bats in the belfry and dew on the moor, with a chorus you can easily imagine drifting like peat smoke from the bar in a small Irish village, when *bonhomie* has long since turned to maudlin memories.

It was that streak of Irish melancholia – the flip side of the Celtic coin of boisterousness – that first drew Waits to The Pogues. "You have to give them awards for standing up first of all ..." Waits admiringly reported. "They're like something out of a Hieronymous Bosch painting ... The singer's got a smile like the South Bronx." Waits also admitted that his daughter Kelly Simone's favourite record is The Pogues' version of Ewan MacColl's 'Dirty Old Town'.

Separated by the Western Ocean, Tom Waits and The Pogues are nonetheless kindred spirits. Waits was all set to produce the band's third album, but contractual problems with The Pogues' label intervened and the consequent three-year delay between albums evidently clashed with Waits' commitments. Waits had even taken copies of The Pogues' second album 'Rum, Sodomy And The Lash' back as presents for his *Ironweed* colleagues Jack Nicholson and Meryl Streep, but sadly their response remains unrecorded.

Pogues accordionist James Fearnley has vague memories of a wasted evening with Waits during the Chicago run of *Frank's Wild Years*. Cruising a series of increasingly cheesy Chicago bars, with Waits' name opening all manner of dubious doors, Fearnley dimly recalls playing the theme from *Exodus* accompanied by Waits on the piano.

Waits' mother was also in town at the time, to see how her only son was getting on with his career, probably delighted that he appeared to have gone 'legit'. Somehow she had been inveigled into joining the pub crawl, prompting her son to remark from the stage at the bitter end of the evening: "I can't believe it, my mother drinking in a bar with The Pogues."

Former Pogues bassist Cait O'Riordan (now Mrs Elvis Costello) had first sung with a North London band called Pride Of The Cross, they only cut one single: 'Tommy's Blue Valentine', a tribute to Cait's hero, Tom Waits.

'Frank's Wild Years' is Waits' best album of the decade, a masterly mélange, veering wildly from vindaloo bite to milksop innocence. Even without the linking thread of Frank, the songs have a real cohesion and they display some of Waits' best ever writing; in these lyrics he proved again his unusual ability to convey honest sentimentality whilst never allowing it to become stomach-turning nostalgia. Frank Leroux's odyssey had trailed over four years and Waits had grown fond of the character, but now it was Frank, RIP.

"'Frank's Wild Years' closes a chapter, I guess. Somehow the three of 'em seem to go together; Frank took off in 'Swordfish', had a good time in

'Rain Dogs' and he's all grown up in 'Frank's Wild Years'. They seem to be related – maybe not so much in content, but at least in terms of being a marked departure from the albums that came before ..."

For Waits, the whole 'Frank' experience had marked an opportunity for him to mount a crusade, to pursue a vision of bringing the accordion back to the forefront of American popular music. Waits' fondness for the instrument went right back to his teenage years, he once claimed that his first professional engagement was as first accordion with a Polish polka band back home in Pomona. One of the featured accordionists on the 'Frank' album was Los Lobos' David Hidalgo, who had also performed the same task on Paul Simon's 'Graceland'.

Waits wanted the album of 'Frank's Wild Years' to be full of textures, he wanted it to sound like Braille. The problem facing him was, that as the technology-obsessed eighties progressed, attaining a rough grain was proving more and more difficult. Waits' affection for archaic instruments like the Optigon which he used on the album's 'Straight To The Top (Rhumba)' and 'Temptation', has been well documented; he explained to Bill Forman: "The Optigon is kind of an early synthesizer/organ for home use. You have these discs that give you different environments – Tahitian, orchestral, lounge – and then you apply your own melodies to those different musical worlds. It comes with a whole encyclopedia of music worlds."

Waits also retained a great and perverse fondness for the Mellotron, which in the eyes of most people had long since been made obsolete by the synthesizer. Unfortunately as Waits himself admitted, his passion for these instruments often turned into a technological nightmare when he tried to record them: "The Beatles used the Mellotron a lot. Beefheart used it a lot. They're real old and they're not making them any more. A lot of them pick up radio stations, CB calls, television signals and airline transmitting conversations. And they're very hard to work with in the studio because they're unsophisticated electronically. So it's almost like using a wireless or a crystal set.

"Most of the instruments ... can be found in any pawnshop," Waits admitted. "I haven't completely joined the 20th Century. I sing through a $29.95 police bullhorn, and once you've used one of those, it's hard to go back! There's something about the power it commands and the authority it gave me in the studio over musicians."

This was his third outing as producer, and Waits admitted that he could be "a real bastard" in the studio: "Everybody has to wear a uniform with their name on it. If they're paid well, you can expect just about anything from them. It's an army. Runs on its stomach. Or we run on your stomach." In the same vein, Waits nominated as one of the highlights of the recording sessions, seeing "Bill Schimmel, classically trained at Juilliard, on his hands and knees, playing the pedals of the B-3 organ with his fists. Working up a sweat!"

With Frank preserved on vinyl for posterity, Waits turned his thoughts to how he could get back on the road, still with elements of the *Frank* show on board. He was characteristically evasive at this time about his relationship with the musicians in his touring band: "The basic economics of touring kept me in tow ... The new band is all midgets, they share a room, they don't want to be paid for their work. They all have a basic persecution complex and they want me to punish them for things that have happened in their past life ...'"

One of the first people Waits had approached for help in bringing *Frank* to life was director and scriptwriter Jim Jarmusch, with whom Waits had intended to collaborate on a script for *Frank's Wild Years*, but it never came about. Instead Jarmusch got Waits on board for his second feature *Down By Law*, which he described encouragingly as a "neo Beat noir comedy"; besides giving Waits his biggest part to date, the film included the songs 'Jockey Full Of Bourbon' and 'Tango Till They're Sore' from the 'Rain Dogs' album on its soundtrack.

The main reason, Waits swore, that he was so keen to appear as Zach, the down-and-out disc jockey in Jarmusch's film, was that he got to wear a hairnet. Jarmusch kept the hairnet in as an enticement and spoke to *Q* magazine about his star: "Tom's a very contradictory character in that he's potentially violent if he thinks someone is fucking with him, but he's gentle and kind too. It sounds schizophrenic, but it makes perfect sense once you know him. He's a fine actor too. I learned a lot from him, and yeah, he really likes to get dressed up, which is good, 'cos he puts on different clothes and becomes a different person."

Down By Law was deeply, deeply flawed. Jarmusch was just too eager to let his characters find their own way out of situations, often allowing the camera to dwell on them in the hope of something happening. Consequently there was no real development of the relationships and this gave an uneasy feeling of inertia to the whole film. Waits was memorable as Zach, but the film was stolen by Italian comedian Roberto Benigni, whose total grasp of the English language at the commencement of filming was restricted to the word 'hello'! "Ees a sad anna beautiful world," announces Benigni to Zach, slumped with a bottle, a bad liver and a broken heart, to be greeted with Waits' response "Buzz off." "Buzza off. Thank you very much. Buzz off. It's a pleasure."

The film kicks off with some moody, monochrome shots of New Orleans and Tom Waits getting nine different types of shit kicked out of him by Ellen Barkin. Waits' character comes across like someone out of one of his own songs, rootless and questing, hat perched precariously as he sets off tilting at windmills.

Early on, Zach dreams of getting back on the air. Despite the failure of his attempts at communication with Ellen Barkin, he is somehow still convinced that he can communicate when he's broadcasting. But we know that he'll never get the chance again, that he's condemned instead to a lifetime listening, of hearing streetcars rattle through the soft, mint-julep night on their way to Desire Boulevard.

Zach's downfall comes when he's asked to deliver a car to the other side of town. There he is, cruising along at the wheel, quietly slewed, singing along in cracked accompaniment to Roy Orbison's 'Crying', when he's flagged down by the cops. Instead of the the spare tyre and wheel-jack normally found in car boots, there's a still-warm stiff.

Once stuck inside the prison the film flags, and even after they've escaped out on to the Bayoux, the three-way relationship between Waits, Benigni and Lounge Lizards' saxophonist John Lurie never really develops. Fugitives from the chain gang movies had been in more capable hands with Paul Muni, Paul Newman and even Woody Allen; while edgy buddy-buddy relationships had been handled better by Jack Nicholson and Mickey Rourke. Ultimately, *Down By Law* fizzles rather than frazzles. But yes, without a doubt, Waits was right to go with the hairnet.

By 1987, the Waits family had relocated to Los Angeles: "For what I used to pay to park in New York, I bought an apartment in Los Angeles"; and so it was in LA that Waits put his tour band through a rigorous 16-hour-a-day rehearsal period before going on the road to promote 'Frank's Wild Years'. Unfortunately Waits had too many bitter memories of thankless support slots and rigorous headline tours throughout the seventies for him to have any fondness left for life on the road: "I couldn't even laugh at *Spinal Tap*. It was too real for me. That film's every tour I've ever been on. I didn't laugh once. I wept openly!"

For the 'Frank' tour there was a set that looked like the 'Used Carlotta' Waits had envisaged all those years ago. It was a junkyard that looked like it was home to the neighbourhood derelicts. Waits would also take an occasional solo on the working fridge that featured prominently stage right. Fridges weren't witnessed in many rock shows, but Waits eschewed dry ice and stuck instead with the fridge. He'd also recruited a band that were as tight as a Pogues audience on St Patrick's Night – percussionist Michael Blair, guitarist Marc Ribot and keyboard maestro Willie Schwarz in particular shone.

The bulk of the set was drawn from 'Swordfishtrombones', 'Rain Dogs' and 'Frank's Wild Years', although Waits did unforgettably reacquaint us with 'Tom Traubert's Blues' and 'Christmas Card From A Hooker In Minneapolis'. Those 1987 shows demonstrated just how far Waits had

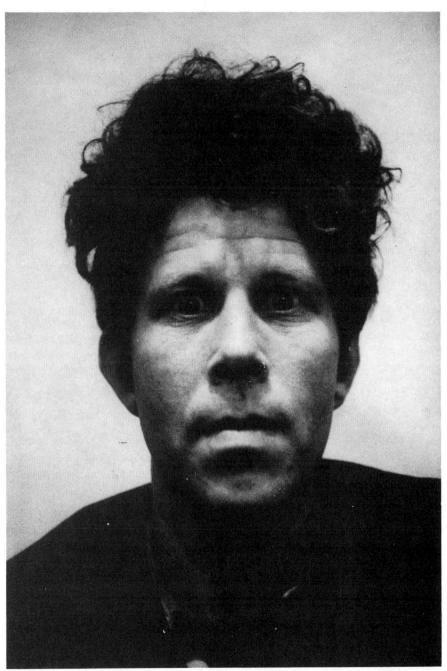

Peter Anderson

With Meryl Streep (left) and Jack Nicholson in Ironweed   *Palace Pictures*

The beatnik, early 1970's.   *LFI*

Peter Anderson

Rain Dog on the prowl in New York.   *Peter Anderson*

Barry Plummer

Waits considers alternative career in the months before Bruce Springsteen covered 'Jersey Girl'.

LFI

Peter Anderson

travelled, how much he'd learnt and how magnificently he could put it all together.

Despite a voice that was as intimidating as hell, when Waits sat down and sang about the Christmas card he'd received, he was utterly believable. That same voice was capable of quite extraordinarily subtle nuances as he chronicled the lives of the people he'd created. The mistake he had made early on in his career of becoming those types was now replaced by a sympathy with, and fondness for, them. Like a scientist in the laboratory of his imagination, Waits watched as his creations scuttled round the stage. There was both exotic mystery and down-home nostalgia in these songs. Powered by thunderous percussion, injected with a colourful leavening of sitar and accordion, Waits' songs were orphans coming home, and here was Waits greeting them with open arms.

Here also was the humour, as always an integral part of the show. Waits was never afraid of taking a pratfall on stage, he wasn't a performer who needed to be loved, only his characters needed that. Not for Waits the ersatz "really great to be back at your wonderful Hammersmith Odeon ..." routine. The audience could laugh at the incongruous sight of him in a tuxedo doing his best to croon; at the idea of Tom Waits, of all people, trying to kid you that if his voice hadn't been shot to hell, he could sing like Frank Sinatra. They knew that 15 years of assault and battery on his nodes had ensured that it was only a dream he was chasing.

Waits kept himself busy pushing the idea of the performer on-stage to its limit. You couldn't imagine Bryan Ferry singing through a police bullhorn, or really believe that Waits felt closer to his audience than his immediate family, but it was fun anyhow. Taking the audience even further into his confidence, Waits coyly confessed that the question he was most frequently asked was: "Can I get pregnant without intercourse?"

Waits' reputation preceded him on his travels around the world, and wherever he went he seemed to meet characters that were straight out of his songs: "I met a guy one night," he told Chris Roberts, "came up to me with his hand out, I said 'Oh no', he said 'Hey listen, it's not what you

think, I don't want any money, I just wanna be your friend, my name is
Charlie, what's your name?' I said 'My name's Tom.' He said 'How ya doin'
Tom, that's all I wanted, see ya.' He went all the way around the block,
came all the way back, saw me coming round the corner and said 'Hey
Tom, it's your old buddy Charlie, can you loan me a coupla bucks?' I got a
kick outta that."

Maybe Waits hadn't made it straight to the top, it had after all been a
slow and haphazard journey to somewhere half-way up the greasy pole of
success. But even if they haven't yet named a street after him, among
those who have testified to his influence are Elvis Costello, Nick Cave,
Tanita Tikaram, The Pogues, Bruce Springsteen, REM, Robin Williams,
Nanci Griffith, John Stewart, Keith Richards (on the sleeve of his solo
début, Keef acknowledged Waits' 'spiritual encouragement') and U2. The
Edge admitted, "I love Tom Waits. I think he's the great talent of the last
10 years as far as dealing with America in a real way."

Elvis Costello told me: "I've always admired Waits, we used to stay in
the motel he lived in in LA – a nodding acquaintance literally – as he'd be
passing by with his groceries." Elvis went on to explain that Waits was one
of the first choices as Master of Ceremonies for his 1987 Wheel Of Fortune
Tour with the Attractions: "The whole idea of the Spinning Wheel thing
was that I have a very large repertoire, and you can never satisfy the
demands of your audience, even if you play three and three-quarter hours
... So I thought how can I get myself off the hook? I'll invent this Wheel
thing, so it's not my fault if it's a matter of chance ... I had in mind various
people for the character of Napoleon Dynamite the MC. Over the course
of the tour we had the Italian Sam Fox, Roberto Benigni who came up and
translated everything I said into nonsense: I'd say 'I'd like someone to
come up and spin the wheel' and his translation would be 'He prefers snow
to ice cream!'

"We began the Wheel shows in LA and I asked Waits to come and co-
host with me. He was remarkable, he coined a lot of the expressions which
ended up in the show. We had a roving spotlight and he was prowling
around the front of the stage and picked out this voluptuous girl in the

audience and growled, 'I knew you were out there, baby', then went on with some story that she was a dancer he knew from Vegas."

Waits and Costello were also down to collaborate on the *NME*'s imaginative 'Sgt Pepper Knew My Father' album in 1988, on which contemporary artists such as Billy Bragg, Sonic Youth and even The Fall recreated The Beatles' classic 'Sgt Pepper' album track for track in the same sequence as the original. Tom and Elvis were keen to work together on an acoustic version of the album's climactic 'A Day In The Life', but sadly schedules clashed, and the task fell to The Fall. Elements of Waits' cut-up technique found their way onto Costello's acclaimed 1989 album 'Spike', which also featured Marc Ribot and Michael Blair from Waits' band.

The only way Tom Waits could've got on to the stage at *Live Aid* was by offering to sweep it, but in September 1987, he was among the first to be asked by Musical Director T-Bone Burnett to guest at Roy Orbison's testimonial at Hollywood's Coconut Grove. Alongside Bruce Springsteen, Elvis Costello, Jackson Browne, James Burton, k.d. Lang and Jennifer Warnes, Waits came out to pay tribute to The Big O (Waits had once facetiously claimed to have been Orbison's babysitter). In the audience, Leonard Cohen, Billy Idol, Dennis Quaid, Harry Dean Stanton and Richard Thompson were among those who marvelled at the all-star circus running through Orbison's best-loved songs. The ensuing video reveals guitarist James Burton's look of incredulity at Waits' stumbling 'solo' on 'Ooby Dooby'.

Orbison's death, on December 6, 1988 aged 52, was not only tragically premature but ironic in its timing. After years in the wilderness, Orbison was back on a roll as a member of the all-star Travelling Wilburys, while a strong new solo album featured guest appearances by U2 and Elvis Costello. *Rolling Stone*'s obituary of Orbison, included a touching testimonial from Tom Waits: "Roy Orbison's songs were not so much about dreams but more like dreams themselves, like arias. He was a ghost coming out of the radio. His songs will not be diminished by his passing, for he was a rockabilly Rigoletto, as important as Caruso in sunglasses and a leather jacket. Roy's songs always sounded like they were trying to reach out to you from far away. When you were trying to make a girl fall in love with you, it took roses, the Ferris wheel and Roy Orbison. His songs will haunt us always."

Waits has never been one for hangin' out with the right crowd just for the sake of it. When he began his professional career in the early seventies, star jams and guest appearances were *de rigeur*: Joni and 'Willy'; Stephen and Judy; James and Carole; Jackson and Linda, it was like some Californian musical dating agency gone mad, but it was not for Waits. He confided in 1974: "I drink heavily on occasion and shoot a decent game of pool and my idea of a good time is a Tuesday evening at the Manhattan Club in Tijuana. I reside now in the Silver Lake area of Los Angeles and am a dedicated Angeleno and have absolutely no intention of moving to a cabin in Colorado. I like smog, traffic, kinky people, car trouble, noisy neighbours, crowded bars and spend most of my time in my car going to the movies."

Tom Waits as corrupter of youth was another role he relished, delightedly recalling a letter he had once received from a kid in the mid-West who had been suspended from school for bringing in a Tom Waits album for his class project!

Waits had largely created his own character. He had made himself into the forlorn figure in Edward Hopper's 'Nighthawks', the fly on the face of rock's ever-increasing pomposity, the wordsmith who got drunk on dictionaries. He was the madcap laughing at the folly of mankind, who could tug at your heartstrings with a ballad dredged from the very depths of his soul or leave you smiling wryly at the onslaught of one-liners. He got under your skin and left you scratching. He proved that you can fart and chew gum at the same time. Waits was the idiot savant, he was Beat writ large, he was sensitive soul cast low.

Some of rock music's most haunting and affecting songs have come from Waits' pen. He is a master craftsman when it comes to composition, but in conversation is rarely less than evasive. Throughout his career Waits has been colourful and entertaining on the vexed subject of the creative process, but poker-faced he fends off more probing questions about the nuts and bolts of songwriting.

When Barney Hoskyns asked him how he sits down and writes, Waits responded: "What I usually do is I write two songs and I put 'em in a room together and they have children. I have to start with two. I don't write year round, I write like a season and then I'm done. I would like to be able to write through it all, but ... it gets hard, so you say I'm gonna set this time aside and for me a lot of it's like going back to a place where you go a lot, but the season changed and the vines grew over the entrance ... and you get back there and you say well I'm standing right where I was, how come I can't get back in ... and then you realise that things grew over and then you get through that and you see the little path and then you're on your way ...

"When the writing season finishes? Oh, I entertain guests; I'm a member of the Junior Chamber of Commerce; I do bus tours round New York; I repair lamps; I play golf. Nah, if golf was really a part of my life ... I think I'd put sunglasses and a raincoat on and sneak off to do it at night!"

Waits is a great believer in the ability of the popular song to travel, so that for example, 'Waltzing Matilda' functions as the chorus of 'Tom Traubert's Blues' without the seam showing. His great respect and fondness for the founding fathers of American popular music: Stephen Foster, the Gershwins, Cole Porter, Hoagy Carmichael etc is also well known and their influence can be heard on much of his early work. Waits had repeatedly proven his ability to work within the recognised format and now he had staged his very own Destruction Derby on the structure of the songs for 'Swordfishtrombones'; on that album, the songs themselves were made to struggle for air.

"Every song is special," he told Ann Scanlon. "They're like birds, you send them out there: some of them get blown out of the sky on the first day, some of them come back, some of them go across the country. You don't always know what's going to happen: who's going to sing them, who's going to hear them. I still believe in the way that stories and jokes travel and I like to think about songs in terms of mythology – you're sending something out and that should be able to transcend the machinery of business."

Waits' air of facetiousness when talking about his work belies the perspiration and inspiration which goes into his craft: "My music is kinda like tabasco. You can use it on fish, fowl or poultry. See, I really only listen to 'em to if they're ready, then I send them off running out into the street. Like chickens. Some come back and stay with you; some disappear. It's kinda like a shipwreck with all these things floating on the water."

In his excellent book of searching interviews with rock songwriters *Written In My Soul*, Bill Flanagan found Waits in lurid and revealing form. Beneath the usual snappy one-liners and opaque metaphors, Waits clearly prides himself on his abilities, but is equally aware of his limitations: "When you're writing your life is like an aquarium. Some things float and some things don't. Some things breathe and some drown. Some look better and some worse. That's the moment I know I'm writing – when I've filled the room with water ... It's like the little crane with the claw in the arcades. You always go for the radio or the watch but you never get it. It weighs too much. You end up with those little wax candies and a couple of rocks ...

"Songs are kind of like hats. I look good in this now, maybe I won't tomorrow. But right now I've had a couple of drinks and the hat feels good. Recording is so permanent it's maddening. I enjoy the whole process until we get to the end and they say 'Tom, we're going to have to finalise this.' I hate that. Up till then it's like a rehearsal, I don't like the end of it 'How do you want your nose, Tom? We're going to break it and reset it and move your cheek there. Remove the lower lip altogether. You're just going to have a chin and teeth. We'll find a way to lock 'em in. Now we're going to shave your head, put watches all up and down your arm, and send you to Passaic for a couple of nights and have you photographed. How do you feel about that Tom?' 'Well, uh, I don't know ...' So they drug you and put you in a car and ...

"Some songs you have to hit over the head, drag home, skin, cook and eat. Every song has a life expectancy. Some songs you play only once and that's it ... There's one song, 'Time', that I can't even play any more. It happened that one time and I haven't been able to get it back ... Any attempt to recreate that moment is like showing pictures of your family. The pictures never really capture what happened: 'Here I am with Mrs Chalmer. You'd love Chalmer, he's here with Evelyn. And there's Elwood! You can't see all of Elwood, he's behind Ruby. And here's Howard. Well ... You had to be there'."

The disillusionment with the music industry that Waits had felt at the end of the seventies had been partly banished by the triumphant reception accorded to 'Swordfishtrombones', 'Rain Dogs' and 'Frank's Wild Years'. The transition to Tom the Thespian had helped too.

Waits is one of the few 'rock stars' to make it to the big screen without the raspberry being blown. Is there some small print in recording contracts that says if you sing then you have to act too? Was it blackmail that got Mick Jagger cast as Ned Kelly? Was David Bowie under a death threat when he mugged his way through Merry Christmas Mr Lawrence? Was Roger Daltrey fully conscious when he read the script of Lisztomania? Didn't Bob Dylan see 'Turkey' writ really large on the script of Hearts Of Fire?

Maybe it was the pernicious power of promo videos that made pop stars into mummers. Just filch some images made memorable by classic movies, pump in plenty of dry ice and get your singer to stand around looking moody. It may have filled up the three minute slots on MTV, but A Streetcar Named Desire it wasn't.

While Waits hasn't yet scaled the cinematic heights achieved by Kris Kristofferson or Bette Midler, he does have an impressive show reel. His truncated performance in The Cotton Club had registered and he made the most out of the morass that was Down By Law.

The **Big Time** could be heard calling across the swamp of ambition when Hector Babenco was casting the follow-up to his Oscar honoured *Kiss Of The Spider Woman*. A coupla promising kids called Jack and Meryl were already on the menu, what Babenco and writer William Kennedy were looking for now was some bum to play a deranged character called Rudy the Kraut ...

CHAPTER SEVEN

Both Dennis Hopper and Harry Dean Stanton had already been tested for the role of Rudy in *Ironweed*, but author William Kennedy had his own ideas. Waits knew the author from the time they spent together while filming *The Cotton Club*, Kennedy had been one of many writers called in to knock the film into shape and had ended up sharing the finished screenplay credit with Coppola.

"I ran into him again at a black tie affair in San Francisco," Waits recalled to Ann Scanlon. "He said to me, 'Boy, you oughta play Rudy', and I said 'Well, Goddam, but I don't know. They're probably thinking of some big shot for the part, somebody with more experience, and I'm very unconventional ...' I went to New York, met Nicholson, and read with him. I had some toast and an old toothbrush sticking out of my pocket, hadn't shaved, my hair was all messed up and I guess the director and everyone liked it pretty good. They even gave me the costume when the film was wrapped up – so I got a new suit out of it!"

This was it for Waits, time to sit at the grown-ups table, co-starring alongside multi-Oscar winners Jack Nicholson and Meryl Streep in a mainstream movie backed by a major studio. Filming began in February 1987 and Waits' relationship to Nicholson's character was crucial to the film's success. Alongside such seasoned pros as Carroll Baker and Fred Gwynne, Waits' inexperience would be further highlighted if he failed.

William Kennedy's novel was the concluding part of his 'Albany Trilogy' and on its publication in 1983, *Ironweed* had won the Pulitzer Prize. Kennedy was fulsome in his praise of Waits and the way in which he brought Rudy to life: "Rudy is a crazy character, a kind of lost soul who has pickled his brains in whiskey and wine, and Tom was perfect for the part. From the way he wears his hat to the way he sits around, he can play the crazy, loopy bum wonderfully well. He tried out in the presence of Jack Nicholson and everyone realised what great chemistry there was between these two guys. Tom's a natural; a terrific actor."

Director Hector Babenco had found himself at the helm of a surprise hit with his 1985 *Kiss Of The Spider Woman*, the film which also gained William Hurt his first Oscar. After sifting through innumerable treatments and screenplays looking for a suitable follow-up, Babenco finally settled on Kennedy's novel as the basis for his first Hollywood project.

Kennedy's story about drifters and derelicts at the tail end of the Great Depression was, on the page, a powerful tale, but it failed to translate to the screen. Nicholson and Streep look like they're slumming it purely in the pursuit of 'versatility', and surely one of the cinema's most redundant credits to date has to be Alba Censoplano as 'Ms Streep's Costumer'.

At the heart of the film is Nicholson's lifetime of agonising over the death of his baby son as a result of his drunkenness, the tragedy which first propelled him into the life of a hobo. His partner in the skid row flop-houses is Rudy, a buoyant performance from Waits. Rudy provides some much needed light relief during the 135 minutes of otherwise undiluted gloom. Even though he's dying of cancer, it's still a question of who'll go first, Rudy or his shoes.

Despite the film's determinedly authentic recreation of 1938 Albany, despite Nicholson's grittily convincing portrayal of Francis Phelan and despite director Babenco's reverential handling of Kennedy's script, *Ironweed* just doesn't cut it.

There are distinguishing moments, Babenco's handling of a night-time raid on the hobo camp is flawlessly shot, and the scenes where Nicholson pitifully endeavours to regain the bosom of his estranged family are touching. But finally, too little actually happens over the two-and-a-quarter hours, and the audience is left marvelling at the authenticity of Nicholson and Streep's wardrobes rather than caring about the future of their characters.

Whatever the flaws of the film as a whole, Tom Waits excels, proving himself a dramatic match for Jack 'n' Meryl. He invests Rudy with a dignity which manages to make the character rise above caricature, Waits looks and sounds the part. It is his most convincing performance to date, it's only a shame that a more worthwhile vehicle wasn't afforded him.

123

Jack Nicholson was also impressed with his co-star, commenting: "At rehearsals, Tom Waits looked like at any moment he might break at the waist or his head just fall off his shoulders on to the floor. I once saw a small-town idiot walking across the park, totally drunk, but he was holding an ice-cream, staggering, but also concentrating on not allowing the ice-cream to fall. I felt there was something similar in Tom."

Waits was, predictably, rather more elliptical when considering his colleague: "Jack's real, he's very worldly, very wise. One minute he's like a captain of industry, and the next he talks like a railroad bum ... He'll eat out of a can, but he also enjoys watching dog shows ... Meryl Streep? Gothic and devastating. There was great chemistry, because he's mostly mischief and she's mostly discipline, so it makes a little old-fashioned relationship."

From an unpromising film début in the 1958 Roger Corman cheapie *The Cry Baby Killer*, Jack Nicholson has reached the very pinnacle of American film acting. After four Oscar nominations, Nicholson finally got to take the little gold man home for his unforgettable performance in 1975's *One Flew Over The Cuckoo's Nest*. Waits eulogised to Bill Forman about his co-star: "Nicholson's a great American storyteller. When he tells a story, it's like a guy soloing, he's out, you know? Very spontaneous, thinks on his feet. I remember he said 'I know about three things: I know about beauty parlours, movies and train yards'."

The craft of acting was something that Waits felt he had to develop slowly and by observation: "I guess great actors work in the same way as writers in the sense that you compose a character from different parts of yourself: somebody else's limp, your grandmother's dentures, your brother-in-law's posture and your catechism teacher's dialect."

Waits had few hopes that his own contribution to life, music or the movies would be honoured. Still waiting to be ennobled by the Academy of Motion Picture Arts And Sciences, he told *Playboy*: "I'm not big on awards. They're just a lot of headlines stapled to your chest, as Bob Dylan said. I've only gotten one award in my life, from a place called Club Tenco in Italy. They gave me a guitar made out of a tiger eye. Club Tenco was created as an alternative to the big San Remo Festival they have every year. It's to commemorate the death of a big singer whose name was Tenco and who shot himself in the heart because he'd lost at the San Remo Festival. For a while it was popular in Italy for singers to shoot themselves in the heart. That's my award!"

From third-billing, Tom Waits moved into 1988 with his name above the title. Nestling up to 40, Waits was finally headed for the *Big Time*. Plans for filming the stage version of *Frank's Wild Years* had been shelved, but Waits and his wife were now doubly keen that something should be preserved of the ensuing tour.

Asked once to define show business, Groucho Marx had reminisced: "We were playing a small town in Ohio and a man came to the box office and said 'Before I buy a ticket, I want to know one thing, is it sad or high kicking?' To me that's it – 'sad or high kicking'."

Big Time was both sad and high kicking, but neither the film nor the soundtrack album really demonstrated the full variety of the live show. Missing were Waits' diverting monologues. Live albums are notorious for being used as stopgaps by established acts: stymied at following up 'Tommy', The Who filled in, quite admirably as it happened, with 'Live At

Leeds'; his career in periodic abeyance, Bob Dylan has released a series of increasingly lack-lustre live sets; unwilling to consider even attempting to top 'Born In The USA', Bruce Springsteen, probably the most bootlegged live rock performer of all time, offered not one but five albums worth of live material.

With his inimitable reputation as a live performer, Tom Waits had not been well served by 'Nighthawks At The Diner'. 'Big Time' should have delivered, but came back marked 'Return To Sender'. With an obvious reliance on his eighties work, 'Big Time' added little to the extant studio versions. The only new song was the leaden, country-sounding 'Falling Down', which had Waits coming across as a revivalist at a riverside John Ford gathering.

'Strange Weather' which Waits had written with his wife Kathleen, was chosen by Marianne Faithfull as the title song for her most recent comeback album. Producer of the 1987 album was Hal Willner, who also put together 'Lost In Stars', the Kurt Weill album tribute in 1985 and the widely acclaimed 1988 Walt Disney testimonial 'Stay Awake', both of which featured a contribution from Waits. Marianne Faithfull was a label-mate of Waits at Island, and he had originally been scheduled to work with her on her new album, suggesting at one point that all the songs should have a 'Storyville' theme: Storyville was the red light district of New Orleans where jazz had been born. But like so many others, the Storyville concept was stillborn.

As a *bona fide* film star, Waits had his own image of himself, which the reality of the finished film didn't always match. "I see things about myself and the show I don't like. I thought I was much taller, for example, I thought I looked like Robert Goulet or Sean Connery. It was really shocking to see this old guy sweating, bending over and scratching his head. It was a rough night." But he soon grew accustomed to the sight of himself as the star in his own film, and slowly his confidence crept back: "I realise now why they were thinking of me as the only man capable of replacing James Bond."

Later he was to claim that the whole film had been shot in one day for $100 and that all the scenes with Faye Dunaway were cut out! "*Big Time* is a kind of action-adventure movie, one guy in Chicago said piano teachers will be shocked, someone else said it looked like it was filmed in the belly of a very sick animal ...''

Rock concert films are notoriously unreliable creatures. The Rolling Stones' 1981 world tour was rock's most lucrative ever, but the subsequent film *Let's Spend The Night Together* stiffed; even U2's *Rattle And Hum* has only been seen by a tiny percentage of the fans who bought the album by the lorry load. There are of course exceptions to the rule, among them Talking Heads' *Stop Making Sense* and Prince's *Sign O' The Times*, and to these, for all its flaws, can honourably be added Tom Waits' *Big Time*.

Eschewing the archetypal concert movie clichés, Waits and director Chris Blum were shooting at stars with *Big Time*. The audience never appeared, the camera was locked on all the Tom Waitses parading before it. There was Waits as the huckster theatre usher ("Wanna buy a watch?"), the insincere, so sincere crooner ("I feel closer to you than my whole family") and the final shot of Frank singing 'Innocent When You Dream' from inside a shower on a Los Angeles rooftop, surely a cinema first this?

The Frank filmed here is a loser, a character for whom the *Big Time* will always remain just a dream; like the old gag about the guy whose job is to be blown out of an elephant's arsehole every night in the circus. Afraid that it's making him ill, he goes to the doctor and is told he'll have to give up the job for the sake of his health, only to respond "What? And give up show business!"

As Frank the Crooner, Waits is at his most convincing, just the merest smidge of a pencil-thin moustache giving him the air of a Sleaze King, the sort of guy who'd auction his in-laws as a tax loss. The white tuxedo is visual shorthand for a self-centred, slimy, showbiz worm, the sort of character who'd make out an autograph 'With sincere good wishes to my very dear friend ...' and then ask, 'What did you say your name was again?'

Holding centre-stage throughout the film's course, Waits was totally mesmerising. On 'Way Down In The Hole', he dispenses lines like saliva from the mouth of a Hellfire and Damnation preacher. On 'Straight To The Top' his pastiche of a nightmare Vegas entertainer lays bare all the falsity and hypocrisy of the industry, and makes you think that if "There's no people like show people," then God help us all.

Wielding the bullhorn like a baton, Waits marshals his troops; Willie Schwarz in his fez looking like he's on his way to audition for the bad guys in *Lawrence Of Arabia*, saxophonist Ralph Carney on his back sending notes soaring off into the upper circle. But always it's Waits who holds your eye. Illuminated by a cheap lightbulb, he looks older than his 39 years, but then he always has looked as though he's just stopping off *en route* to the old folks' home.

At times his movements are cumbersome, like the mangled mazurka in the middle of 'Rain Dogs'; then again he can be fluid as a stroboscope. He sounds like a 78 rpm record winding down, but then again he can reach into your heart and set you marvelling at the poignancy of his reading of 'Johnsburg, Illinois'.

There is much to admire and enjoy in the finished film. The live version of 'Hang On St Christopher' put me in mind of Waits' views on other Saints: "St Moritz, the patron saint of all hotel night clerks; Susan St James; St James Infirmary. There's 'The Saint', Roger Moore, of course ..."

When *Big Time* goes off-stage though, it gets patchy. The image of Waits singing '9th And Hennepin' underneath a flaming umbrella is memorable, but it suggests that he may have fallen victim to the disease of video directors: taking a memorable image, and placing it in isolation, thereby signifying naught. I wished that *Big Time* had opened out more, Waits is clearly blessed with a strong eye for visual absurdities, just check out his line in grisly sunglasses if you need any further proof. Even allowing for its abundance, *Big Time* begged for more, and what exactly lay behind that very mysterious end credit "featuring Gertz the Monkey"?

With a career stretching back over 15 years and with the experience gained from starring in hundreds of shows, a Tom Waits concert film should have been able to capture what James Grant of Scottish band Love And Money had in mind, when he said that a Waits concert was: "like seeing a pantomime, a horror film and a gig all in one evening." But sadly it wasn't quite like that.

Waits recognised the weaknesses of *Big Time*. Following its release he told Jonh Wilde: "It's just a concert film ... It's certainly not fiction ... It looks to me like an old shopkeeper yelling at some kids to get away from his store ... It's difficult to retain what happened at that moment and preserve it. You don't want to kill the beast while you're trying to capture it. Also, the moment after it's completed you'd love to go back and change something. Like watching my underwear come out of the back of my pants."

Even putting the *Big Time* album and film to one side, 1988 was still a busy time for Tom Waits. His contribution to 'Stay Awake – Various Interpretations of Music from Vintage Disney Films' – was hailed as one of the album's highlights. The album also featured Waits' favourite band of the moment, The Replacements: "They like distortion. Their concerts are like insect rituals," and Buster Poindexter (aka the New York Dolls' David Johansen, whose Buster persona owes more than a nod to Waits' own).

Other contributions on 'Stay Awake' came from Ringo Starr, Sinead O'Connor, James Taylor, REM's Michael Stipe and 10,000 Maniacs' Natalie Merchant; but it was Waits' idiosyncratic version of 'Heigh Ho', the dwarfs' marching song from *Snow White And The Seven Dwarfs*, which was repeatedly singled out.

Project overseer Hal Willner saw Waits' interpretation as ... "a protest song, I think that Tom felt that the dwarfs really didn't want to go to work, and his version reflected that." It was certainly hard enough to reconcile the bright, breezy image of the happy-go-lucky dwarfs in the Disney film with Waits' chain-gang rendition on 'Stay Awake'. In the *Big Time* film, Waits had maintained that the two missing dwarfs were "Friendly and Snooty", and if there's time, I'd like to squeeze in my favourite Snow White story too. An amateur production which could only muster five dwarfs, saw Snow White standing stage-centre surrounded by her somewhat diminished entourage, ad-libbing to the non-existent pair off-stage: "Now you two stay behind and tidy up the cottage for when we get back!"

Waits has been openly scathing about rock stars who align themselves to advertising campaigns: "I really hate the people that do them," he told

Ted Mico. "I've been asked to endorse everything from underwear (lightning resistant) to cigarettes. I turned them all down. They cut bacon off your back before the pig is a ham. A lot of people go to Japan to do it, as though you can shit in the desert and no one will know. The lines are drawn, they have to be as advertising is aligning itself with new counter-cultures. It puts decals on all your work. The idea is to be sovereign independent and not to have to work on 'Maggie's Farm', but there are people who should know better buying into a piece of the rock with assholes like Bob Hope. Why do you want that kind of money? It's money that uses you as a sperm to fertilise the egg of industry!"

The eighties has seen corporate sponsorship play an increasingly dominant role in rock music, with established acts such as George Michael, The Police, David Bowie, Tina Turner, Madonna and Michael Jackson allying themselves to brand names. Their proffered justification is that sponsorship offsets the high costs of touring, therefore enabling them to keep their ticket prices down, thereby acting as a service to their fans. What it has really meant is that fans have felt betrayed by the idols they created, who now appear willing to sacrifice every vestige of independence and dignity on the altar of Mammon.

129

It doesn't seem very likely that either Pepsi or Coca-cola will be rushing to Tom Waits' door, bidding for his services to help bolster their product. Mind you stranger things have happened; who could have imagined that punk poet John Cooper Clarke would one day be seen promoting the benefits of a certain brand of breakfast cereal on children's TV. But with advertising's increasing reliance on plundering pop history, everything and everyone was up for grabs.

In 1977, Waits had been mildly chuffed to learn that Rowlf The Dog on TV's The Muppet Show bore more than a passing resemblance to his own persona, but in 1988 he was incensed when Salsa Rio Doritos Corn Chips began a series of radio commercials using a character right next to Tom Waits at the bar. Waits responded with a two million dollar lawsuit, alleging that the company "Wrongly and without justification, appropriated ... (his) singing style and manner of presentation." The wheels of American justice grind exceedingly slowly, and it may be years before a decision is reached. It profits a man nothing to give his soul for the whole world – but for corn chips?

'Big Time' was Waits fourth album for Island, and to help celebrate the label's 25th birthday in 1988, he sent a taped message to label boss Chris Blackwell expressing his delight that Blackwell had given up the midget wrestling outfit and gone into showbiz! Island have given Waits plenty of encouragement and support during his time with them, they even put out a half-hour video compilation in 1987 which had Waits musing on such topics as clocks, confetti and exactly where barbers went to get their hair cut.

Interviewed in the back of a limo, Waits gave hell to Wayne the chauffeur, cradled a seedy looking poodle called Mario and made first base in interview. "Five words to describe yourself?" "No left turn!" "Favourite country?" "St. Louis!" "Future plans?" "I live for adventure, and to hear the lamentations of the women."

Barely pausing to draw breath, Waits finished up the year by starring in two further films. *Candy Mountain* was a feature from Robert Frank, director of the largely unseen Rolling Stones documentary *Cocksucker Blues*. Frank was also a noted photographer of the Beat era and had taken the back cover photo on 'Rain Dogs'; coincidentally, he was also responsible for the cover photos of Waits' favourite Rolling Stones album 'Exile On Main Street'. The story for *Candy Mountain* was by Rudy Wurlitzer, who had previously scripted Sam Peckinpah's elegiac *Pat Garrett And Billy The Kid*. In the film, Waits played a wealthy music business mogul with a big cigar, a house in New Jersey and a penchant for golf. Waits had initially been down for a bigger part but his commitments to *Ironweed* over-ran and as a consequence, his role in *Candy Mountain* became little more than a cameo.

Robert Dornheim's *Cold Feet* had Waits as a hit man from Florida with a great wardrobe, starring alongside Keith Carradine and the splendidly named Rip Torn. On location in Bizbee, Arizona, waiting to film the last scene about smuggling a horse with a hollow leg across the Mexican border, Waits had plenty of time between takes to swap yarns with actor and singer Keith Carradine whose song 'I'm Easy' from Robert

Altman's memorable 1975 movie *Nashville* had won that year's Oscar for Best Original Song.

While on location, Waits shared his views on acting with Mark Goodman, as he settled down to his 12th film: "Movies are done in such small segments that you have to be very careful about preparation in order to stay in character, to be ready; you can't really sit around and watch the world news. It's like a very large orchestra, and you're one of the members; and since it's a director's medium, he's the conductor, the one you have to trust. You don't ever sincerely leave the ground the way you do in a performance on-stage."

Waits and Carradine got on well together while filming on location. Between takes, Carradine would entertain the cast and crew with theatre stories, like: "So this tenth-rate actor is doing *Hamlet*, and he's so bad that by the time he gets to the soliloquy, the audience is booing, throwing filthy vegetables at him. Finally, halfway through the soliloquy, he stops and turns to the seats and says, 'Hey, look, I didn't write this shit!'"

Early 1989 found Waits making his legitimate straight acting début in a new play *Demon Wine* in Los Angeles. Starring alongside Carol Kane and Bud Cort (the baby-faced oddball from the cult 1971 black comedy *Harold And Maude*), Waits collected a fistful of favourable reviews.

It has been two years since an original album of Tom Waits material; *Frank's Wild Years* marked the end of an era which had begun four years before, and where the Waits trajectory will take him next is only known inside his cranium.

For over 15 years, Waits has kept his career sizzling like eggs on a griddle; he has avoided consistency, evaded being pigeonholed and in addition has produced 11 albums of original material which manage to defy description but remain powerful statements of a maverick talent. Initially out of step with the marshmallow soft-rock of the early seventies, Waits' career veered off at a tangent as he persevered down the mean streets and unlit alleys, beret at the ready. Swerving between dour low-life reportage and exhilarating flights of fancy, Tom Waits always follows his own roller-coaster muse.

131

Among Waits' best songs are his anthems for the dispossessed, testaments for those who must fight not to be ground down by an uncaring society; they are songs for those forever stuck 'on the nickel'. If, as I suspect time will prove, Michael Douglas' Gordon Gekko becomes the enduring symbol of Thatcherism and Reaganomics, with his insistence that "Greed is good", then Waits' songs are as good an antidote as any to that specious but pervasive argument.

The characters he trawls in his music are underdogs, marooned and hapless in a world where everything's broken. There was a time when Waits looked like he would fall victim to his own myth, but he's grown out of that. Now he's no longer looking at the world over a bottle of Bushmills, now he's a benevolent father of two, dispensing wit and wisdom, coping with the age-old problems of raising children in a world that's out of control, tired of trying to explain the disparities, but persevering.

Diehards of the Waits image of the seventies find it hard to reconcile with the contented family man, cosy in his domestic bliss, happier changing nappies than dispatching yet another bottle of tequila to the bottle bank. On learning that Waits and his family were in Dublin while they were performing there, The Pogues looked forward to a repeat performance of their Chicago encounter in 1986. Quitting the stage just before midnight, they made it back to the hotel anticipating an evening of Bacchanalia with the Crown Prince, only to learn that Waits had retired to bed hours before.

The currency of the man's work just keeps rolling along. While finishing this book, I watched a BBC *Everyman* programme about a group of Vietnam veterans who had returned to Vietnam 20 years after they served in the army there. The trip took them to Saigon (now Ho Chi Minh City) and to Hanoi; while there they saw the new victims of America's saturation bombing, tiny babies born years after the war had ended, but still suffering the pernicious effects of the Agent Orange defoliant, the belated legacy of napalm. Chastened, the vets returned to their hotel where their scratch band was later seen pumping out a ragged version of Waits' '(Looking For) The Heart Of Saturday Night'. Something in the lines about 'the magic of the melancholy tear in your eye' struck home, a song Waits had written 15 years before found fresh resonance in a hotel bar in the heart of Vietnam.

And the future? "The last few albums have had more optical illusions in them. They were less linear, less conventional. I tried to use some techniques to blur the edges. The songs were more out of focus. I was trying to give them nervous breakdowns ... I'm trying to take a hammer to what happened. Don't hold a mirror up to it. Hit it with a hammer. Take my advice."

You won't get an inkling by discovering what Waits has been listening to lately, his favourite album of recent years is apparently a field recording: "'The Romiyiana Monkey Chant' ... This guy went into the jungle and found a group of natives that sat ritualistically in concentric circles and did what has come to be known by millions as the Romiyiana Monkey Chant, where they relive their own tribe being saved by monkeys ... These monkeys apparently came down out of the trees and killed an attacking tribe. Romiyiana. Ask for it by name. Accept no substitutes."

133

In the late spring of 1989, Waits spent a month in Hamburg with Robert Wilson, writing the score for Wilson's play *The Black Rider* described as 'a cowboy opera'. "There'll be seven principal players," Waits revealed. "All the rest will be carrying spears. It's a little oblique."

Waits' collaboration with Wilson also brought him together with 75-year-old Beat guru William S. Burroughs. It was Burroughs who coined the phrase 'heavy metal', watched Steely Dan and The Soft Machine lift their names from his works, appeared on the cover of 'Sgt. Pepper' and taught David Bowie all he needed to know about the cut-up technique and less. A seminal influence and author with the best-stocked arsenal in New York, Burroughs first met Kerouac in 1944 and cropped up periodically in the Kerouac canon, as 'Old Bull Lee' in *On The Road*, 'Frank Carmody' in *The Subterraneans* and 'Bill Hubbard' in *Desolation Angels*.

Beyond that Waits speculates: "When I'm an old guy, I'll sit on the porch with a shotgun and a skirt, and an umbrella, and if you hit your baseball in my yard you'll never see it again ... Kansas is a good place to dream. You wake up in the morning, look out the window and don't see anything, you make it all up."

But that's what Tom Waits has been doing all his professional life. One thing for certain is that we're unlikely to see Tom Waits featured on 'Lifestyles Of The Rich And Famous' or find him seated at a piano in a Vegas auditorium simpering "Here's an old tune of mine that you might remember ..." No. The Tom Waits that'll always cause a wry smile or a poignant pause is the old groaner slumped at his piano in some lowlife den, picking at the ivories and plucking at your heart strings.

There'll always be a fragment of an album that can cause a pause in the course of life, a meandering anecdote from a favourite concert, the strangely shy interviewee trying to unravel the complexities of the world and weave a better sort of truth.

Fingers as white and bony as the ivory he plays, eyes fixed on some distant dream, he is trying perhaps to recall that lost innocence and relay it to his own children. "Any advice for your daughter?" asked Kristine McKenna. "That you can dream your way out of things and into things. And I don't mean being in a lousy place and pretending you're somewhere else. I think you can dream yourself out of some place and into another place that's better for you. To dream hard enough; I hope I can teach her how to do that."

PEOPLE TOM WAITS WOULD GIVE FLOOR SPACE TO:

Lord Buckley, Lenny Bruce, Harry Partch, The Pogues, Jack Kerouac, Charles Bukowski, Nelson Algren, Francis Ford Coppola, Howlin' Wolf, The Drifters, Sam and Dave, The Temptations, James Brown, Edward Hopper, Nick Ray, Victor Feldman, Harry Dean Stanton, Jack Nicholson, Bruce Springsteen, Chuck E. Weiss, Mose Allison, Wally Cox, Harry 'The Hipster' Gibson, Symphony Sid, Cole Porter, Nat King Cole, Frank Sinatra, John McCormack, Prince, Roy Orbison, Elvis Costello, Miles Davis, Keith Richards, Agnes Bernelle, George and Ira Gershwin, Jerome Kern, Steve Allen, Harold Arlen, Bud Powell, Charlie Parker, Thelonious Monk, Martin Mull, Willy De Ville, Little Walter, Ray Charles, Wilson Pickett, Cleo Laine, Kurt Weill, the Seven Dwarfs, Hanns Eisler, Louis Armstrong, Kathleen, Kelly and Casey ...

TEN REAL BOOKS TOM WAITS WOULD ENJOY READING

How To Avoid Intercourse With Your Unfriendly Car Mechanic – Harold M. Landy (Ashley Books, 1977)

Octagenarian Teetotallers, With 113 Portraits – Anon (National Temperance League, 1897)

Fifty New Creative Poodle Grooming Styles – Faye Meadows (ARCO Publishing, 1981)

How To Abandon Ship – Philip Richards and John J. Banigan (Cornell Press, 1942)

Proceedings On The Second International Workshop On Nude Mice – Anon (University of Tokyo, 1978)

I Knew 3,000 Lunatics – Victor R. Small (Rich and Cowan, 1935)

On Sledge And Horseback To Outcast Siberian Lepers – Kate Marsden (The Record Press, 1892)

Premature Burial And How It May Be Prevented – William Tebb and Edward Perry Vollum (Swan Sonnenschein, 1986)

Bread Making In Scandinavia In The Early Middle Ages – Agneta Lundstrom (Almquist and Wiksell, 1976)

Manhole Covers Of Los Angeles – Robert and Mimi Melnick (Dawsons, 1974)

TEN REAL AUTHORS TOM WAITS WOULD WELCOME ON HIS GUEST LIST

Ludwig Von Baldass

Ellsworth Proutyconkle

Manfred Lurker

Professor A. Moron

Curt Redslob

James Patrick Sex

I. I. Shitts

Negley King Teeters

Morten Thing

Sabrina Wurmbrand

SOME INSULTS TOM WAITS WOULD RELISH:

"Don't talk to me about writing, you couldn't write 'fuck' on a dusty Venetian blind." Coral Browne.

"Well, maybe I could *initial* it ..." Tennessee Williams, on being asked to autograph a drunk's penis.

"If I ate alphabet soup, I could shit better lyrics than that." Johnny Mercer.

"He's about as much use as a one-legged man at an arse-kicking contest." Liverpool expression.

"You have Van Gogh's ear for music." Billy Wilder to Cliff Osmond.

"I didn't like the play, but then I saw it under adverse conditions – the curtain was up." Groucho Marx.

"He'd use the skin of his mother to make a drum to sound his own praises." Margot Asquith on Winston Churchill.

"He looks like the guy in a science-fiction movie who is first to see The Creature." David Frye on President Ford.

DISCOGRAPHY

ALBUMS:

CLOSING TIME (1973) Asylum SYL 9007, reissued Asylum K53030, 1976: Ol' 55; I Hope That I Don't Fall In Love With You; Virginia Avenue; Old Shoes (And Picture Postcards); Midnight Lullaby; Martha / Rosie; Lonely; Ice Cream Man; Little Trip To Heaven (On The Wings Of Your Love); Grapefruit Moon; Closing Time (Instrumental).

THE HEART OF SATURDAY NIGHT (1974) Asylum K53035: New Coat Of Paint; San Diego Serenade; Semi Suite; Shiver Me Timbers; Diamonds On My Windshield; (Looking For) The Heart Of Saturday Night / Fumblin' With The Blues; Please Call Me, Baby; Depot, Depot; Drunk On The Moon; The Ghosts Of Saturday Night (After Hours At Napoleone's Pizza House).

NIGHTHAWKS AT THE DINER (Double Album) (1976) Asylum K63002: Opening Intro; Emotional Weather Report; On A Foggy Night; Eggs And Sausage (In A Cadillac With Susan Michelson) / Better Off

Without A Wife; Nighthawk Postcards (From Easy Street) / Warm Beer And Cold Women; Putnam County; Spare Parts I (A Nocturnal Emission) / Nobody; Big Joe And Phantom 309; Spare Parts II.

SMALL CHANGE (1977) Asylum K50350: Tom Traubert's Blues (Four Sheets To The Wind In Copenhagen); Step Right Up; Jitterbug Boy (Sharing A Curbstone With Chuck E. Weiss, Robert Marchese, Paul Body And The Mug And Artie); I Wish I Was In New Orleans (In The Ninth Ward); The Piano Has Been Drinking (Not Me) (An Evening With Pete King) / Invitation To The Blues; Pasties And A G-String (At The Two O'Clock Club); Bad Liver And A Broken Heart (In Lowell); The One That Got Away; Small Change (Got Rained On With His Own .38); I Can't Wait To Get Off Work (And See My Baby On Montgomery Avenue).

FOREIGN AFFAIRS (1977) Asylum K50368: Cinny's Waltz (Instrumental); Muriel; I Never Talk To Strangers (duet with Bette Midler); Medley : Jack And Neal, California, Here I Come; A Sight For Sore Eyes / Potter's Field; Burma Shave; Barber Shop; Foreign Affair.

BLUE VALENTINE (1978) Asylum K50388: Somewhere (from *West Side Story*); Red Shoes By The Drugstore; Christmas Card From A Hooker In Minneapolis; Romeo Is Bleeding; $29.00 / Wrong Side Of The Road; Whistlin' Past The Graveyard; Kentucky Avenue; A Sweet Little Bullet From A Pretty Blue Gun; Blue Valentines.

HEARTATTACK AND VINE (1980) Asylum K52252: Heartattack And Vine; In Shades; Saving All My Love For You; Downtown; Jersey Girl / 'Til The Money Runs Out; On The Nickel; Mr Siegal; Ruby's Arms.

BOUNCED CHECKS (1981) Asylum K52316: Heartattack And Vine; Jersey Girl (alt. master); Eggs And Sausage; I Never Talk To Strangers; The Piano Has Been Drinking (Live) / Whistlin' Past The Graveyard (alt. master); Mr Henry (previously unreleased); Diamonds On My Windshield; Burma Shave; Tom Traubert's Blues.

ONE FROM THE HEART (1982) CBS 70215: Tom's Piano Intro; Once Upon A Town *; The Wages Of Love *; Is There Any Way Out Of This Dream? *; Picking Up After You *; Old Boyfriends *; Broken Bicycles / I Beg Your Pardon; Little Boy Blue; The Tango; Circus Girl; You Can't

Unring A Bell; This One's From The Heart *; Take Me Home *; Presents (* featuring Crystal Gayle).

SWORDFISHTROMBONES (1983) Island ILPS 9762: Underground; Shore Leave; Dave The Butcher (Instrumental); Johnsburg, Illinois; 16 Shells From A Thirty-Ought-Six; Town With No Cheer; In The Neighbourhood / Just Another Sucker On The Vine (Instrumental); Frank's Wild Years; Swordfishtrombones; Down, Down, Down; Soldier's Things; Gin Soaked Boy; Trouble's Braids; Rainbirds (Instrumental).

ASYLUM YEARS (Double Album) (1984) Asylum 960321-1: Ol' 55; Martha; Rosie; Shiver Me Timbers; San Diego Serenade / Diamonds On My Windshield; (Looking For) The Heart Of Saturday Night; The Ghosts Of Saturday Night (After Hours At Napoleone's Pizza House); Small Change (Got Rained On With His Own .38); Tom Traubert's Blues / Step Right Up; Burma Shave; Foreign Affair; Mr Henry; The Piano Has Been Drinking (Not Me) / Potter's Field; Kentucky Avenue; Somewhere (from *West Side Story*); On The Nickel; Ruby's Arms.

RAIN DOGS (1985) Island ILPS9803: Singapore; Clap Hands; Cemetery Polka; Jockey Full Of Bourbon; Tango Till They're Sore; Big Black Mariah; Diamonds And Gold; Hang Down Your Head; Time / Rain Dogs; Midtown (Instrumental); 9th And Hennepin; Gun Street Girl; Union Square; Blind Love; Walking Spanish; Downtown Train; Bride Of Rain Dog (Instrumental); Anywhere I Lay My Head.

LOST IN THE STARS (1985) A&M AMA5104 – Waits only featured on one track – 'What Keep's Mankind Alive'.

FRANK'S WILD YEARS (1987) Island ITW3: Hang On St Christopher; Straight To the Top (Rhumba); Blow Wind Blow; Temptation; Innocent When You Dream (Barroom); I'll Be Gone; Yesterday Is Here; Please Wake Me Up; Frank's Theme / More Than Rain; Way Down In the Hole; Straight To The Top (Vegas); I'll Take New York; Telephone Call From Istanbul; Cold Cold Ground; Train Song; Innocent When You Dream (78).

BIG TIME (1988) Island ITW4: 16 Shells From A Thirty-Ought-Six; Red Shoes; Cold Cold Ground; Way Down In The Hole; Falling Down; Strange Weather / Big Black Mariah; Rain Dogs; Train Song; Telephone Call from Istanbul; Gun Street Girl; Time.

STAY AWAKE (1988) A&M AMA3918 – Waits only featured on 'Heigh Ho (The Dwarf's Marching Song)'.

SINGLES:

Somewhere/ Red Shoes By The Drugstore
Asylum K12347 1979

In The Neighbourhood/ Frank's Wild Years
Island IS141 1983

Downtown Train/ Tango Till They're Sore
Island IS253 1985

Downtown Train/ Tango Till They're Sore/ Jockey Full Of Bourbon
Island IS235 (12″) 1985

NME'S BIG FOUR (1986) NMEGIV3 – Waits featured alongside The Jesus And Mary Chain, Husker Du and Trouble Funk, on a special 'NME version' of 'Downtown Train'.

In The Neighbourhood/ Singapore
Island IS260 1986

In The Neighbourhood/ Singapore/ Tango Till They're Sore (live)/ Rain Dogs (live)
Island ISD260 (7″ double pack) 1986

In The Neighbourhood/ Jockey Full Of Bourbon/ Tango Till They're Sore (live)/ 16 Shells from A Thirty-Ought-Six (live)
Island IS12260 (12″) 1986

Hang On St Christopher/ Hang On St Christopher (instrumental)
Island 096750 (12″) 1987

16 Shells/ Black Mariah (live)
Island IS370 1987

16 Shells/ Black Mariah/ Ruby's Arms (live)
Island IS370 (12″) 1987

GUEST APPEARANCES:

'Homeplate', Bonnie Raitt (1975) Warner Bros KS6160 (UK) BS2684 (US), Waits piano/backing vocals.

'I'm Everybody I've Ever Loved', Martin Mull (1977) ABC AB997 (US), Waits guests as barman on one track, 'Martin Goes And Does Where It's At'.

'Broken Blossom', Richie Cole (1980) Muse MR5207. Waits appears at end of one track, 'Waitin' For Waits', explaining he had to stop for a Chinese meal before the session.

'Dirty Work', Rolling Stones (1986) Rolling Stones Records CBS86321 (UK), Waits guest vocalist and piano on 'Harlem Shuffle', also released as 7″ single (RSA6864).

Aficionados of Tom Waits and his ouevre will find Frank's Wild Records at 19 St Martin's House Parade, The Bull Ring, Birmingham, B5 5DL, an Aladdin's Cave of Waitserie.

COVER VERSIONS OF TOM WAITS SONGS:

IAN MATTHEWS: 'Some Days You Eat The Bear ... And Some Days The Bear Eats You' (1974, Elektra) 'Ol' 55'; same version included on 'Best Of ...' compilation 'Discreet Repeat' (1980, Rockburgh).

THE EAGLES: 'On The Border' (1974, Asylum) 'Ol' 55'.

TIM BUCKLEY: 'Sefronia' (1974, Discreet) 'Martha'.

BETTE MIDLER: 'Songs For The New Depression' (1976, Atlantic) 'Shiver Me Timbers'; live version appears on her 'Divine Madness' (1980, Atlantic).

ERIC ANDERSON: 'Be True To You' (1975, Arista) 'Ol' 55'.

JACK TEMPCHIN: 'Jack Tempchin' (1977, Arista) 'Tijuana', co-written with Waits, otherwise unavailable.

MANHATTAN TRANSFER: Extensions (1980, Atlantic) 'Foreign Affair'.

RICKIE LEE JONES: 'Girl At Her Volcano' (1983, Warner Bros) 'Rainbow Sleeves', Waits never recorded this song; Jones' version was also included on soundtrack of *The King Of Comedy* (1983, Warner Bros).

ENGLISH COUNTRY BLUES BAND: 'Home And Deranged' (1983, Rogue Records) 'Tom Traubert's Blues'.

PAUL YOUNG: 'The Secret Of Association' (CBS, 1985) 'Soldier's Things'.

BRUCE SPRINGSTEEN: 'Jersey Girl', live version as B-side of 12" single 'Cover Me' (1984, CBS); Springsteen also used live version of song as finale of his five-album 'Live 1975-1985' (1986, CBS).

T-BONE BURNETT: 'T-Bone Burnett' (1986, MCA) 'Time'.

BEAT FARMERS: 'The Pursuit Of Happiness' (1987, Curb) 'Rosie'.

MARIANNE FAITHFULL: 'Strange Weather' (1987, Island) 'Strange Weather'.

PATTI SMITH: 'Downtown Train' (1987, CBS single).

DION DIMUCCI: 'Yo Frankie' (1989, Arista) 'San Diego Serenade'.

FILMOGRAPHY:

PARADISE ALLEY (1978): Directed by Sylvester Stallone. Starring Sylvester Stallone, Kevin Conway, Anne Archer.

WOLFEN (1981): Directed by Michael Wadleigh. Starring Albert Finney, Gregory Hines, Edward James Olmos.

ONE FROM THE HEART (1982): Directed by Francis Ford Coppola. Starring Frederick Forrest, Teri Garr, Raul Julia, Nastassia Kinski.

THE STONE BOY (1982): Directed by Chris Cain. Starring Robert Duvall, Glenn Close, Frederick Forrest.

THE OUTSIDERS (1983): Directed by Francis Ford Coppola. Starring Matt Dillon, Emilio Estevez, Patrick Swayze, Rob Lowe, Tom Cruise, Ralph Macchio.

RUMBLE FISH (1983): Directed by Francis Ford Coppola. Starring Matt Dillon, Mickey Rourke, Dennis Hopper, Diane Lane.

THE COTTON CLUB (1984): Directed by Francis Ford Coppola. Starring Richard Gere, Bob Hoskins, Fred Gwynne, Diane Lane, Gregory Hines.

DOWN BY LAW (1986): Directed by Jim Jarmusch. Starring John Lurie, Ellen Barkin, Roberto Benigni.

IRONWEED (1987): Directed by Hector Babenco. Starring Jack Nicholson, Meryl Streep, Carroll Baker, Fred Gwynne.

BIG TIME (1988): Directed by Chris Blum. Starring Tom Waits.

CANDY MOUNTAIN (1988): Directed by Robert Frank. Starring Kevin J. O'Connor.

COLD FEET (1989): Directed by Robert Dornhelm. Starring Keith Carradine, Sally Kirkland, Rip Torn.

Omnibus Press
No.1 for Rock & Pop books.

Omnibus Press and Bobcat Books have published books on the
following rock and pop stars:

AC/DC ... Bryan Adams ... A-Ha ... The Alarm ... The Beatles ... Pat
Benatar ... Chuck Berry ... Big Country ... Black Sabbath ... Marc Bolan
... David Bowie ... Boy George & Culture Club ... Kate Bush ... Eric
Clapton ... The Clash ... Phil Collins ... Elvis Costello ... Crosby, Stills &
Nash ... The Cure ... Dead Or Alive ... Deep Purple ... Def Leppard ...
Depeche Mode ... The Doors ... Duran Duran ... Bob Dylan ...
Eurythmics ... Bryan Ferry & Roxy Music ... Fleetwood Mac ... Frankie
Goes To Hollywood ... Peter Gabriel ... Marvin Gaye ... Genesis ...
Jimi Hendrix ... Human League ... Billy Idol ... Julio Iglesias ... Michael
Jackson ... Mick Jagger ... The Jam ... Japan ... Billy Joel ... Elton John ...
Howard Jones ... Quincy Jones ... Journey ... Joy Division ... Judas Priest
... James Last ... Led Zeppelin ... John Lennon ... Madness ... Madonna
... Barry Manilow ... Marillion ... Bob Marley ... Paul McCartney ... Gary
Moore ... Jim Morrison ... Ozzy Osbourne ... Jimmy Page ... Pink Floyd
... The Police ... Elvis Presley ... The Pretenders ... Prince ... Queen ...
Quiet Riot ... Ratt ... Lou Reed ... Rolling Stones ... David Lee Roth ...
Rush ... The Sex Pistols ... Sigue Sigue Sputnik ... Simon & Garfunkel ...
Simple Minds ... Siouxie & The Banshees ... Slade ... The Smiths ...
Bruce Springsteen ... Status Quo ... Cat Stevens ... Sting ... Supertramp
... Talking Heads ... Tears For Fears ... Thompson Twins ... Pete
Townshend ... UB40 ... U2 ... Ultravox ... Van Halen ... The Velvet
Underground ... Wham! ... The Who ... Stevie Wonder ... Paul Young ...
Frank Zappa ... Z Z Top.

Omnibus and Bobcat titles on all the above are available from good
book, record and music shops. In case of difficulty, contact
Book Sales Ltd., Newmarket Road, Bury St. Edmunds, Suffolk IP33 3YB.